CAVU TO: TOM MITTLER

FROM: Dick WARD.

31 AUGUST 2005

Flying Thoughts - An Aviator's Flight Through Life

by
Richard I. Ward

authorHOUSE™

1663 LIBERTY DRIVE, SUITE 200
BLOOMINGTON, INDIANA 47403
(800) 839-8640
WWW.AUTHORHOUSE.COM

First published by AuthorHouse 05/26/05

ISBN: 1-4208-4920-4 (sc)

Library of Congress Control Number: 2005903765

Printed in the United States of America
Bloomington, Indiana

This book is printed on acid-free paper.

READER COMMENTS

"The "Flying Thoughts" of Dick Ward is a wonderful mix of aviation lore and life's lessons and the author's knack for creative solutions to real life problems both business and personal. We can all benefit from Dick's proclamation "I've been lucky – and the harder I work, the luckier I get." I highly recommend "Flying Thoughts" to aviators and non-aviators alike."

    Steven E. Dyer, President
    Univair Aircraft Corporation

"The book is wonderful! Dick and Donna Ward's life story is interesting, fun and uplifting. This is a wonderful book about a man and his family who succeeded in so many ways. It will be appealing not only to the aviation enthusiast, but to those who love success stories and the interesting experiences associated with them."

    John L. Parish
    Staggerwing Museum Foundation

"As I read Dick Ward's book, it was like he was saying "Come fly with me;" and I did just that. "Flying Thoughts" is written in an interesting and authentic way that helps one to personally relate with his informative reflections. From the chapters on the "Formative Years" to "Final Landings", one can be encouraged to see how God influences our lives. He shows us that we all have a positive destiny, too."

    Rev. John Booko

"Seldom do I start and finish a book in one sitting. "Flying Thoughts" is filled with great words of philosophy and intertwined with anecdotes and personal stories from an era of aviation that needs to be remembered. I treasure the Author's concepts."

    Dick Wagner
    Wagner Foundation, Ltd.

"Over the years, I have met some of the world's greatest musical entertainers. It is always a thrill for me to be around such individuals. They have that something "Special". That invisible, positive force, that makes you want to be around them, and absorb all that you can. Richard Ward is one of those "Special, Positive Forces". When you read "Flying Thoughts", you will see that Richard also has command of the English language and makes his story, a fun and informative read. Thank you for letting this man take "flight."

Col. Rendal Wall
Heritage Guitar, Inc.

Table of Contents

ACKNOWLEDGEMENTS & SPECIAL THANKS

Highest acknowledgements and special thanks go to Donna Wilson Ward who must have a record for holding the longest leash ever affixed to the collar of any husband, and who provides enough passion and comfort to fill ten lives.

To the three Ward Boys who sacrificed much of my companionship during their early years as youngsters, while their Dad worked his 7-day weeks, for their necessary support. I hope they understand!

To Mildred Lena Benninghoff Ward, my Mother who bought me my first model airplane at age 6 and put up with the likes of me. I wish I had thanked her more before she went west. Hopefully she can read this from on high.

To my Uncle Dick and Aunt Betty who allowed us to share their home as a youth and kept me moving in the right direction while my Mother worked those many long hours to collect her meager salary.

To Bob Biggs, a true friend and early flying buddy who made his final flight a few short months ago.

To my many aviation students, past customers, friends and acquaintances who have touched and fulfilled my life. Some are mentioned in this book; the others know who they are.

To Gregory Ward for his creative artistic work by providing the cover design and finished artwork for this publication.

Finally – to A Power beyond that which can be defined. What a great flight this has been.

PROLOGUE

*As we climb the inclined path of age, our "mind's eye" vision
becomes extremely sharp and more focused.
I find this to be a very useful and entertaining phenomenon.*

By: Author

RANDOM MEMORIES - What awesome power The Almighty provides to each of us as individuals. We are able to collect, systematically assemble, then view in our minds eye, wonderful thoughts, using the random collection of 16 billion cells our brains possess. More amazing is that we have the ability to organize, and then record them in writing for others to see. One of the tricks to making this work though, is to step back, relax and give ones mind a chance to recall. Thankfully, I am at a point in my life that permits this luxury of time. This was not always the case. I'm not complaining, but if the road to success were measured in the amount of hours in a day one puts toward their effort to accomplish their goals, my contribution would most certainly win an award. Did luck enter into my formulas for success along the way? It sure did! The harder I worked, the luckier I got!

I have been on this planet seventy-seven years. Sixty-one of them being embraced with the sheer joy of piloting a vast number of airplane makes and models for over 10,000 flying hours, all the while hop scotching through the eminent challenge of nature's elements surrounding man and flying machine. Not going unnoticed in any way is the continued companionship of my best friend and lover of fifty-five years – Donna Wilson Ward. This beautiful and classy individual issued to me the highest license that one can ever receive. That is, the license to live my life to the fullest. Few men can make a claim such as this. It has provided me with more joyous moments and life fulfillment than any one aviator deserves.

If you are an airman, I am certain that you have experienced meeting an old pilot who may not have held the controls of an aircraft for many years. Didn't you sense an immediate acceptance of that person as a friend, without further exploration? A bond was instantaneously established, as the conversation turned to flying matters. Does this bond come from the love of hearing the roar of an engine on takeoff, the feel of the wind over ones face in an open cockpit flying machine, the sensation of speed, or the weather? The *common bond…* is it any of these things I have mentioned? Perhaps so – but more probably is derived from an intimate secret shared by all airmen, yet discussed by few. We have witnessed writers and orators attempt to explain the experience of flight to the earthling. Our elation is something we wish to verbally share, but alas, always fail to do so. We speak of it in generalities and specifics and still fail to lead the earthling along to become as jubilant as we. How can this be? I submit to you, *this is Religion we share.* A working knowledge of God and His kingdom, viewed only by airman, shared only by airmen, and understood only by airmen. Who can disbelieve when viewing while aloft, the Grand Canyon, the sand dunes of Lake Michigan's shoreline, the rapid buildup of ice on an airfoil, the violence of storm centers, the patience of air traffic control centers, or approach lights looming into view on a 200 foot and ½ mile visibility instrument approach? To guide one's aircraft on high brings us closer to God in many ways, and we aviators cherish this relationship.

Within this writing, I believe my younger aviator brothers and sisters will end the read feeling that they have shared enough of my "Flying Thoughts" to gather a sense of what aviation was like for me starting in the early 1940's and working forward. Many older aviators will most certainly nod their heads and share their own "flying thoughts" in their hard earned solitude.

There is far more to an aviator's life than winging through the air at speeds not normally experienced by earthlings. I hope to reveal some of these events in such a manner that they might be shared with you. I will thread the needle of life and permit you to see how my patchwork quilt of events brought me to where I am today. Hopefully you will find some of the philosophies that I developed useful.

You will note occasional references to a "higher power". To me, that means God. Others may use a different term, but that's OK. If this reference offends you, skip over those sections. It won't offend me in any way. Lest my readers feel the forthcoming contents of this writing will be dripping with religious overtones – have no fear. I have no intention of imposing my spiritual beliefs on anyone. However, I would find it very difficult, if not impossible to describe the corners of my life that acknowledge and embrace a higher power. As this book is being written, I must confess that I am doing so as a reflection upon a very fulfilled life. Hopefully it will prompt each reader to take a few moments from your busy day to survey your own experiences by prompting you to relive a few memories of your own. My jottings herein are random. They sway hither and yon, to be sure, but isn't that the way we live our lives? Nothing ever seems to occur in the exact order in which things are planned, but I find that perfectly OK. Pictures formed in our maturing thoughts become more masterful by the day. A sampling of ones experiences, as they are recalled can be brought together in the corners of our minds providing a beautiful patchwork quilt in our minds eye. Exploring these thoughts can provide us with warmth and comfort during our waning years. I share with you the following notation that I penned many years ago, while viewing our earth from on high. I review the process with comfort more often, as my life moves forward in time!

AN AIRMAN'S PRAYER

*God! Captain of our
universe, as we soar with
you at our side through this
short flight on earth*

*Give us sufficient power to
overcome the drag imposed
upon us by problems we
must face*

*Provide us with positive
lift so that it will offset the
gravity of life's occasional
severe turbulence*

*While we aim toward
tomorrow's horizon, please
aid us by checking our
direction so that we are not
steering a radical course*

*Finally, Oh Lord ... when
we start our descent down
life's glide path, let us touch
down only long enough to
flight plan the next leg of
our journey through time
everlasting*

Amen

By: Author

CHAPTER I
THE FORMATIVE YEARS

God writes the flight plan for our journey through eternity but within reason we must follow it or most certainly we will crash.

By: Author

    I'M NOT CERTAIN when my fascination about flying actually started, but I will tell you that it must have been at a very early age. 1927, the year that Charles Lindberg flew the Atlantic was the year that I was born. The connection pleases me. 1931 had even more meaning! I received and can vividly remember my first airplane ride at 4 years of age while sitting in a wicker seat of a Ford Trimotor in Akron Ohio. We were visiting my Aunt Bertha and Uncle Hut. Now, after all of this time, I've gone full circle, having received my FAA Type Rating in 1994 as a volunteer Captain on the Model 5AT Trimotor - N8419, currently owned and operated by the Kalamazoo Michigan Aviation History Museum. Over 530 hours now show up in my pilot logbook as a Captain, piloting that nostalgic bird. That trip to Akron has another special aviation meaning for me as well. My Uncle Hut, then employed by Goodyear, led me by my hand, while we toured the Goodyear hangar. Housed inside of that huge structure, was the newly completed "Akron Dirigible". My young eyes feasted on the sight. Some time later, I can still picture in my minds eye the massive form of the airship "Akron" as it later flew

1

over my head at about a thousand feet, while I was a very young kid growing up in Pittsburgh, Pennsylvania! In the early 1930's during my very first airline flight from Pittsburgh, Pennsylvania to Johnson City Tennessee, I traveled all alone in a Boeing 247D. Pennsylvania Airlines, later to become Pennsylvania Central, provided me with a permanent memory of the pungent cabin smell from fuel and oil leeching through the fuselage seams of that "modern" bird.

Leaping off my Uncle Spear's six-foot high concrete wall in his back yard with a large black umbrella didn't work too well for we infant aviators, but it was a thrilling flight nevertheless. We never seemed to crash too hard! The smell of model airplane dope or as we sometimes called it "banana oil" - still lingers in the corners of my mind. Dope at that time did not have the sinister meaning as it has now. It was that wonderful substance used to tighten and fill the fibers of the skin covering of both model and full-scale airplanes. How very generous and understanding my Mother was, to permit me to build airplane models on a small desk in our bedroom when I was only 6 years old. To be sure, there was not just the lingering odor of the model cement and dope wafting throughout the house, but an occasional drop of glue would accidentally adorn the desktop from time to time. I never heard a complaint.

A disassembled World War One Jenny aircraft was parked in an isolated barn just up the hill on Pittsburgh's Evergreen Road. This machine provided my fellow junior fighter pilots and me with a huge ration of simulated stick time. The enemy pilots didn't stand a chance with us at the controls. We never knew to whom it belonged. Frankly when we visited the barn we never asked, for fear that we would be denied access. In my minds eye, I can still see and feel that gigantic joystick, when I performed routine takeoffs, loops and of course many a victory roll, as I returned from the war front back to our base on Evergreen Road!

WE FLY

"You know the sudden breathtaking sense of exaltation when your car emerges on the crest of some magnificent headland from which you look for miles out to sea or over billowed rows of

mountains below. What is that sensation? It is a sudden sense of power... a feeling that your human faculties have been miraculously extended... <u>*it is a slight taste of divinity!*</u>

How immeasurably greater this sense of divine exaltation is when gliding high in the heavens, looking serenely down upon the colorful, silent world below! It is a feeling known only to those who have learned from personal experience the tranquil glory of flight.

Those who know the freedom of the airways find in the old paths... a sense of restraint, of suffocation almost... much as the pioneer motorists looked back on the days when they sat in clouds of dust behind plodding teams of horses. Each month they find increasing pleasure in the pathways of the sky... slipping down to bright Havana, to Panama or Peru.

Unless you are too old to readjust your habits to new aspects of life, some day you will fly. Fortunate are those men and women who today recognize that the realm of the skies is offering a fresh lease on life. The blithe spirit of a new renaissance is in the air. It is hard for those who feel it to interpret its significance, though we see the faces of men turned upward, and we see the far places of the earth brought nearer in friendly communication.

The great Tri-motored all-metal planes of 1931 are truly yachts that bring you safety not only as sure as the safety of your yachts upon the sea, but as luxurious and as restful. These new planes free your thoughts from mechanical limitations, just as you are today above the concerns of the engine-room of a steamship.

The pilot and mechanic in their forward control room have every mechanical device necessary for day and night flying in all seasons. Fundamentally the new plane is designed as close to mechanical perfection as possible, with all the strength and extraordinary performance ability for which Ford planes are famous. Beautiful as a jewel, it spreads its wings like burnished silver, to fly with the smooth grace of an albatross over sea, over land, over deserts or arctic wastes."

Author unknown
FORD MOTOR COMPANY AD
Circa 1931

Authors First Airline Flight
Pennsylvania Airlines Boeing 247D
Circa 1934, R. Ward Collection

When I was an infant, my Father, a career U.S. Army Officer, was simply not a meaningful part of my childhood life. Mom carried the full burden of bringing me up after their divorce while I was still a toddler. Neither she nor any of those around us ever spoke ill of him. Fortunately Mom always had a job even during the depression years, working as a Comptometer operator in an office for the Union Switch & Signal, then later on for the Great Atlantic and Pacific Tea Company (A&P). There is little doubt that she deprived herself of most of life's paltry luxuries during those times of depression, helping me pursue my quest for aviation in almost any form.

I was created in 1927, the son of pretty darn good stock, Ivan Walter Ward, with a rich English heritage and Mildred Lena Benninghoff, a good German lady. At that time Mom and my Father "Tommy", as he was called by those who knew him, lived in a bedroom rented from my Aunt Mary and Uncle Carl with their son Frank Ward on Braddock Ave., in Swissvale, Pennsylvania. Cousin Frank, 5 years my senior, treated me then and to this day, as a brother. Why Mom's marriage did not work out is speculation, but it probably had mostly to do with my Father's first love, the U.S. Army. "Tommy" went on to experience his illustrious Army career and ultimately enjoyed the retirement experiences of a full Colonel. He remarried Eleanor, a classy woman from the root town of the Ward side of the family – Johnson City, Tennessee. They produced a set of twins – Alice and Alan, as well as another son, Paul. Alan was later killed in a car accident. Eleanor pretty much went down the same road as my own mother, having been left alone to raise her family. She became an expert at taking in sewing in her home to generate an honest income. An amazing relationship with the Ward side of the family existed then and even to this day. Even though the divorce took place between my Mother and Father when I was still in diapers, this never created family friction. The Ward and the Benninghoff clans co-existed in peace and harmony. I've often thought that this would never be possible today. The simple fact is that the lawyers in our country have made this virtually impossible, with their many adversarial techniques employed between a divorcing husband and wife. Every time a wedge is driven deeper between the two, a new invoice can be rendered. None of that existed in the "honorable" days. I hasten to provide my apologies for this statement to my half brother Paul, who is a successful practicing attorney, but facts at least as I see them, are facts.

In early 1964, Col. "Tommy" Ward passed away. As a complete surprise to me I was advised that I was to inherit 1/3 of the very modest estate of my father, inasmuch as he was then divorced from Eleanor. This meager estate would be divided between myself, my half brother Paul and half sister Alice. It was soon discovered that this amounted to very little in financial value, with a single exception. In the many years during his military service years, Col. Ward had accumulated a vast collection of authentic and ancient Chinese art pieces. 113 Pieces to be exact, and this is not considering the quantities in sets, such as tea sets, etc. These objects were stored for the most part in a garage. Upon arrival to Johnson City, Tennessee to settle this estate, it became obvious to me that these museum quality artifacts would strip the estate of a major portion of its value, when an appraisal took place. It would have been necessary to sell off many of them to pay the tax. Not fair, to be sure, but that's the way it was. Those were the years of radically high government estate taxation. To our pleasant surprise, an interesting thing occurred! Because of the statute of limitations, I feel free to pass along this occasion. A Trust Officer of one of the local banks was handling the estate settlement. He knew all about the art pieces and during a preliminary meeting with the three of us, made an interesting statement, along these lines – "I have to go out of town for the weekend and when I return, I don't want to see any of this Chinese art." The rest was easy. On Saturday, we took a Polaroid camera in hand and photographed the complete collection. There was little doubt that a vast difference in unit values existed but this problem was easily solved, with a literal cut of a deck of cards. The high card got to choose first – and so it went. With no regard to value, but rather only to what each of us would like to have, we made our selections in rotation. It worked like a charm... so much so that I have specified that our own heirs utilize this procedure, when we "go west." It's actually written as part of our will.

As a kid, I was raised as a Baptist, and dutifully went to church on Sundays, but along the way turned Presbyterian. Put a more accurate way, my annual financial dues to this day are faithfully donated to the Presbyterian Church. Donna carries on God's work at our local church in rations that make up for my lack thereof. I have been accused of being a C&E man (Christmas and Easter), but my church going friends have added one more initial. It is now C&E&P man. The "P" standing for potlucks! When there are events with food being served at the church, it is possible that you might see me in attendance, depending upon the occasion. I often half kid about my attending the "Big Church In The Sky", when in reality, I

6

do exactly that. There is not a true aviator alive who does not know what this means. I continually harass friends who are men of the cloth by letting them know in no uncertain terms that I have been "closer to God" more in my lifetime than they can ever expect to be. I go on by insisting that I have my own deal going with the Lord. I'm not certain that they understand but as a courtesy to me, they simply smile and don't argue the point. There is a story that I believe to be true regarding the crew of the Enola Gay piloted by Paul W. Tibbets as they were in the preflight briefing before dropping the atomic bomb on Hiroshima Japan on August 6, 1945. When the Chaplain in attendance queried as to whether they wanted him to pray for the mission, the response was – "Sir, we don't work through middlemen, we go directly to God!" This is my thought exactly. For those who need to rely on a structured religion as they make their way through and fulfill their life, it is a wonderful thing. As for me, I have tried it and find it to be completely unnecessary.

Mom and I eventually moved to Evergreen Road on the North Side of Pittsburgh, Pennsylvania, living in the same house with my favorite relatives – my Aunt Betty and Uncle Dick. Our small bedroom on the second floor had twin beds, a couple of chairs, and a hinged top desk. This was our hangout. We shared the dining room with Uncle Dick, Aunt Betty and Aunt Bertha during mealtimes. Later, when they came along, my cousins Bonnie and Karla joined the dinner table. Things were often done this way, around the depression years. My Aunt and Uncle, for reasons I find hard to understand, never seemed to complain about the smell of model airplane dope nor even when on cold days in their basement I ran a mixture of castor oil and white gas through my cast iron "Sky Chief" model airplane engine. Lord, what a wonderful sound that engine made! How can I ever thank them for that? It was while living on Evergreen Road, at a very young age that I accumulated enough instructional flying hours in a Piper Cub seaplane to finally complete my first solo flight. It had a profound effect on my life. If you are lucky enough to have accomplished the same feat, you will know exactly what I mean!

At the age of 92, Aunt Betty decided to join Uncle Dick in the hereafter one day in May 2001. A celebration of her life was held shortly after her passing, in her modest and beloved Presbyterian

Church, in Mercer, Pennsylvania, where she lived after Uncle Dick died. I was provided with the honor of speaking at that event. You'll see from the following eulogy I presented that day, that gal was much more than a casual Aunt to me.

WHAT ARE SOME OF THE THINGS I THINK OF, WHEN THINKING OF MY AUNT BETTY?

I cannot count the ways!

When reflecting on my many experiences through a virtual lifetime involving exposure to and association with the most delightful Aunt that a person could ever expect to have, it provokes memories of considerably more than an Aunt/Nephew relationship.

This petite 92 year young lady without a doubt established herself as the "Grand Madame" of the Benninghoff clan. She touched the lives of almost everyone she met. This uncanny capability is most certainly limited to a very few. One has to think long and hard to envision many more known individuals who provide a lifetime of service to others in these magnitudes. If one's soul could be defined as their "relationship with other people", Aunt Betty's soul will be present throughout infinity.

Aunt Betty married her lover and best friend, my Uncle Dick, who both somehow survived helping raise the likes of me. All the while she shared this grand gentleman with me in my childhood. He provided stability to my life and a huge ration of his influences must have rubbed off. He was a friend and a good guy, but there was some unexplainable effect that must have occurred during this relationship, since I seem to have turned out somewhat OK, as have our children, Dane, Mark and Greg. Was this an accident? I don't think so. Aunt Betty unselfishly shared not only her home on Evergreen Road with her loving husband, but also with myself, my Mother, Aunt Bertha, (Uncle Dicks Mother) and in the earlier Braddock Avenue days, with Grandpa Benninghoff as well. How profound this is! Aunt Betty said it well, when I queried her one time about the possibility of her getting another spouse a while after Uncle Dick passed away. Her response was - "Why would I? I had the best".

Well, let's see! What are some of the other things I think of? <u>All of my thoughts are not pleasant</u>. Here are a few examples;

1. Sauerkraut – Aunt Betty's favorite meal, was avoided by myself at all costs.

2. Why in the world she would ever get married on Christmas Eve, I'll never understand. This inconsiderate act set the scene for all of the Benninghoff clan, including myself to struggle through the long hours of the night before Christmas, waiting for Aunt Betty and Uncle Dick to celebrate their Anniversary by going out on the town, before finally returning to the Christmas tree. In the German tradition, gifts were always exchanged on Christmas Eve. Obviously Santa could not make his appearance without Aunt Betty nor Uncle Dick. The wait until they both arrived back home was unbearable. Neither one of them will ever be forgiven for this gross oversight in the timing of their marriage.

3. During my youth, while bargaining with Aunt Betty to an impasse on some forgotten issue, it became necessary for me to depart the Evergreen Road estate, by climbing out of my second story bedroom window and jumping off the roof. (I forget where I went, after doing so.)

4. I suppose there are other things that happened of an adverse nature, but they seem to have faded from my long-term memory.

Other than sauerkraut, I declare Aunt Betty's cooking absolutely prize winning in nature. Donna has often stated just how much information in the kitchen she was able to glean, through their beautiful relationship. Though Aunt Betty may not have originated all of these scrumptious delights, she was always willing to provide credit where credit was due. An example of that would be Mrs. Waltz's chocolate cake. To this day, it is still the best. But then there are her more famous dishes including "Aunt Betty's bread & butter pickles" and especially the delightful "Aunt Betty's Crepes" recipe. This latter dish has survived these many years at the Ward household, by becoming a Sunday morning ritual. It is so famous, that it was recently seen on the pages of a number of publications including the December/January 1999 issue of "Taste of Home" magazine.

Benninghoff family reunions were something to behold. There is little doubt that Aunt Betty made this ritual run smoothly. The chow at these events was outstanding.

The German "Turners Club" was a place where Aunt Betty not only performed her Ballerina feats, but families socially gathered there as well.

How many people would allow a kid to stink up the house with model airplane dope or castor oil fuel, without a word of complaint? Aunt Betty did!

I think of "Steve" the pet rooster who attacked cousin Bonnie, then later made his way to the dinner table after a few cutting words from Uncle Dick.

When Uncle Dick went off to the War, Aunt Betty permitted my first airplane, a 1932 Aeronca C2, costing $35.00 to be stored in the Barrick garage while I worked on its restoration. This machine finally made it into the air when my good friend Bob Biggs took over its care and custody while I went off to fly in the Navy.

Boiling clothes and scrubbing them with a hand washboard. They were the good old days.

I often form a mental picture of Aunt Betty sitting on Uncle Dick's lap. This was a constant ritual. What was really going on there, Aunt Betty?

I could go on and on, but not without my expressing this most important point. You will always be in my thoughts, Aunt Betty. Thank you for being a major part of my life.

Now get on with it and enjoy your well-earned reunion with Uncle Dick. Give him an extra hug from me!

Auf Wiedersehen.

The Benninghoff clan provided many positive influences in this writer's young life. There are not enough pages in this book to relay all of the wisdom doled out by these fine folks that provided fodder for my later years. Here's an example! My Aunt Harriet passed away in 1995 at the age of 92. While sifting through some of her old papers, the following hand written poem, penned by her at the young age of 14, shined in my eyes as a bright beacon. H. H. Bennett wrote it. It was this type of sentiment that was embedded within her very soul. Would only the educators of today influence our children where they could produce such individual feelings about our Country.

The Flag Goes By

Hats off!
Along the street there comes
A blare of bugles, a ruffle of drums
A flash of Colors beneath the sky.
Hats off!
The Flag is passing by.

Blue and crimson and white it shines,
Over the steel-tipped ordered lines.
Hats off!
The colors before us fly,
But much more than the flag is passing by.

Sea-fights and land-fights, grim and great,
Fought to make and save the State
Weary marches and sinking ships,
Cheers of victory on dying lips,

Days of plenty and years of peace,
March of strong land's swift increase,
Equal justice, right and law
Stately honor and reverend awe

Sign of a nation, great and strong
To ward her people from foreign wrong:
Pride and glory and honor – all
Live in the colors, to stand or fall.

Hats off!
Along the street there comes
A blare of bugles, a ruffle of drums,

> *All loyal hearts are beating high*
> *Hats off!*
> *The flag is passing by*

While attending my local Rotary Club a few months ago, the following episode was noticed by myself and those sitting at our table. We, as a Rotary group of about 80 persons customarily say the Pledge of Allegiance, a short prayer, and then sing a song such as "America". Four of our local high school seniors were invited to see what the Rotary Club is all about. During the singing of "America", not one of the students opened their mouth! They simply did not know the words. What a terrible shame that certain patriotic traditions are not carried forth by some of our educational institutions.

As a young kid, there was always something going on around the neighborhood. Gosh - what ever happened to: mumblety peg (we always carried a jackknife, even to school), homemade stilts, playing king on the mountain, yo-yo's, a line of kids holding hands and playing "crack the whip," carved rubber band powered paddle boats, willow whistles, baskets made from a peach seed, eating lunch in a tree, kick the can, pitching baseball cards, "flying" a June bug tethered on a thread tied to its leg, kite flying, making a tent with a blanket between two chairs, talent shows put on by the kids or playing marbles. Saturday afternoon at the movie to catch up on the latest chapter of Tom Mix or Gene Autry, developing pictures from the sun, climbing to the top of a limber tree and then riding it down to the ground, catching honey bees in a hollyhock flower without getting stung, and on…and on…and…on…Never was there enough time, nor were there any major costs involved in things we did for entertainment and our own enjoyment. We had absolutely no problem filling our youthful hours with imaginative things.

The current generation probably views my generation's childhood as being unfortunate. It is they who may be the unfortunate ones. They will never be able to experience viewing the mental pictures we were able to form in our minds eye while sitting around the radio listening to the likes of "Jack Armstrong – The All American Boy," or "The Shadow." Then there was "Lights Out", the radio program thriller that came on late at night. Laying in bed in the dark, I could pull in KDKA's powerful radio station through my earphones with my home made crystal set's "cat's whisker" wire properly positioned on the galena crystal. I seem to remember that "Raymond" was the host announcer behind that squeaking door. The "Lights Out" bad guy cutting through the bones of his victim with a hand saw presented a graphic picture far superior to anything depicted on the silver screen today. We loved it! Did it warp my mind? There might be those who think so, but...oh well! The things we did to entertain ourselves took virtually no money. That's good, because there truly was very little of that.

A Saturday ritual as a youngster for me was to spend fifty cents. Here's what it would buy! Two streetcar tokens, each costing a nickel. This got me into downtown and back home. 15 cents purchased a matinee theater ticket at the Lowe's-Penn or Stanley Theater, where I would see not only a movie but also a stage show with whoever might be promoting the picture, such as Judy Garland and Mickey Rooney. The remaining quarter purchased three hamburgers at the White Tower (Lord, were they good), for a nickel each plus a chocolate milkshake served in the huge metal container. It was always procedure to stop by the Pittsburgh Press and watch the papers roll through the production. The production workers would always permit me to wander around inside, unescorted. A stroll into the studio of radio station KDKA would sometimes get me the experience of ringing the three "hand chimes" at station identification time. Maybe once a month, a routine walk through the morgue would let me check out any latecomers. On occasion, I'd visit the old Fort Pitt before it was developed as it is now, to just sit in the ruins and experience how things were back then. I would march along with the British Colonel Henry Bouquet in 1763 as he led his tired men into the walls of the Fort after a major Indian battle, and I never got a scratch!

Indeed today we are living in the electronic age and I have managed this transition in my adult life, but I sure feel sorry that most youngsters in our current generation may never experience some of those simple things in life. Wouldn't it be wonderful if they could? Can we give them a hand in doing so? I think we can and we should. Thinking about it today, I believe we did a pretty good job of teaching conservative values to our own three boys. Patterned after my own upbringing, we did not pay them for doing the routine household chores. That only earned them room and board. The money they received had to be earned the old fashion way. WORK! Today, we are proud to view these successful men, and all of their accomplishments.

I don't recall ever getting an allowance. Funds were derived through a variety of imaginative sources that we as kids dreamed up. One time, our neighborhood gang decided to present a stage show in an empty garage. The admission was 10 cents, and primarily friends and parents dutifully paid their entrance fee and filled all of the seats. After the show, the subject of which has long evaporated from my mind, we inspiring actors all strolled over to the A&P store and made an investment in food and ice cream. I still savor again and again the imprinted thoughts and tastes of the baloney sandwiches that we devoured.

Big money was made during the spring and early summer when the violets and lilacs bloomed. Sales were brisk, as I stood by the side of Evergreen Road with a makeshift sign in my outstretched hand offering a bunch of flowers to passing motorists. Lilacs, taken with permission from the bushes of a kind neighbor, Mrs. Shamming, were colorfully grouped and would sell for 5 cents. Picking violets and offering them by the bunch was much more labor intensive and sold for 10 cents. The supply was never ending, and customers seemed willing to pull over to the curb in their car and make a purchase. Little doubt, I think to myself now, my enterprise probably played some small role in pleasing quite a number of wives or girlfriends who were the recipients of these bouquets. Perhaps it even added a degree of pleasure to some otherwise mundane lives.

My first real paycheck job was for pulling weeds at a commercial nursery garden. It was located about 30 minutes by bicycle from home and the pay was 10 cents per hour. I took advantage of the overtime I could get, but there was no such thing as "time and a half," of course. Lunch was fit for a king with the only investment being some slices of white bread smeared with mayonnaise carried to work in a paper sack. Piled high with leaf lettuce, sliced radishes, and often some onions, the free innards came directly from the gardens we were weeding.

Selling the Saturday Evening Post, mowing lawns and various other means were also used to help pay for room and board and at the age of about 12 or 13, I secured a real job after school with the Felt & Tarrant Comptometer Company. The Comptometer was the first successful manually key driven calculating machine. A short training program was provided and I was instructed on the methods of cleaning and servicing these machines. Contracts with many companies throughout the city were held and on a regular basis, the machines would have to be cleaned, oiled and minor field repairs accomplished on the site of each customer. My first assignment is memorable. I was handed a long list of clients and sent out to go about my work. With my service bag in hand, at about 5:00 PM, I proceeded to the nearest streetcar stop to begin making calls... the first being at one of the steel mills in Carnegie. Each machine was skillfully serviced and I continued on to the next customer via streetcar, then on the next, etc. until the full list of customers were visited. Feeling rather proud that I was successful in efficiently applying my newfound skills, at about 1:00 AM I got back to the office, only to find my boss with a frantic look on his face. "Dick," he queried, "Where in the hell have you been? We've been worried about you." When I explained that I simply worked until the list was completed, he shared some of the blame by admitting that he never meant for me to complete the whole list, but rather meant to work only until about 9:00 or 10:00 PM and continue pecking away at the list the next day. The Comptometer job was good for me, but some time later I was able to secure a full time job working after school in a machine shop for the war effort making recoil rings for 50 caliber machine guns. To this day, I feel pride remembering that I was called into the boss' office, handed a $5.00 bill and was congratulated for the fact that I had produced more parts on my machine in a single 8-hour shift than any other worker. That extra $5.00 was immediately converted into flying time at the Pittsburgh Seaplane Base.

All of this, it seems to me, contributed to my successful business career in the field of aviation and expanded business fields later in life.

CHAPTER II
AIRPLANES & PUBERTY

OH SURE! AS A YOUNGSTER girls were on my mind but by now you can guess what else we kids talked about. I was just 15 years old when I purchased my first airplane. A 1930'S model Aeronca C2. $35.00 was the price! No, that is not a misprint! My lifetime friend Bob Biggs helped me disassemble and haul it from Greensburg, Pennsylvania to be stored in Aunt Betty's garage where I would ultimately start its restoration. The garage was empty and well suited for the assignment, since Uncle Dick enlisted early in the Navy and was off to War. The fact that the airplane was in need of new fabric and an engine overhaul didn't deter me. I was rapidly developing my skills by being enrolled in a fulltime aviation mechanic course offered by South Vocational High School in Pittsburgh's South Side. At my young age, I was already working on the school's Wright Whirlwind, Curtis OX5, and Hispano-Suiza engines. The simplicity of that little two cylinder 36 horsepower Aeronca E-113 engine presented no stumbling blocks whatsoever. If it did, no one ever told me and I accomplished it anyhow. Work did not progress too fast because spare time was at a premium, with my attending school full time and working a full 8 hour night shift on a factory lathe. Shades of WWII! I started but did not complete the rebuild, since I enlisted in the Navy Air Corps. Before shipping out, the C2 was turned over in trust to friend Bob Biggs. He had the work completed by someone else and flew it a while before selling it.

AERONCA C2
CIRCA 1930's
Photographer unknown

Come to think of it, I never saw any of that money, but I think I am still ahead of him. "Biggs" was the only guy in our circle of friends who owned a car, and he never requested money for gas. When I later dated Donna (my wife of 55 years) the choices were to take her on a date using a streetcar for transportation, a method demanded by Donna's strict Gram O'Leary, who raised her, but the other option was to give Biggs a call for transportation. We occasionally opted for the latter. Gram did not seem to mind this, probably assuming that Donna was insulated from my possible advances toward her protected granddaughter with a second guy in the car. Are there still friends like that left in this world?

Pittsburgh had another great asset. It was Al Buck's Seaplane Base. Situated near The Point on the Allegheny River directly under the 6th Street Bridge in the heart of the City of Pittsburgh. It was a beehive of aviation activity, both flying and social. Landings were normally made down river, with each final approach literally taking you between the towers of the bridge. Or for more of a thrill, one could sail over the railroad bridge and slide under the 6th street bridge before touching the water. This became a popular technique when paying flight time by the minute since it took less time to taxi back to the base. This railroad approach commanded an altitude reducing slide slip maneuver, due to the short distance between the two bridges.

I started to haunt this marvelous place from the time I was 15 years of age. My logbook reflects my very first dual instructional flight on April 3rd, 1943. It was 15 minutes long, and my first instructor was Milt Segrist. Immediately thereafter, my instructor was Virginia Givens who later went off to fly with the Women's Airforce Service Pilots (WASP.) How could I afford flying lessons? I really couldn't! But somehow after receiving a pay check from my 8-hour per night machine shop job, and paying my share of our room and board to Aunt Betty, anything left over would make its way to Al Buck's pockets at the seaplane base for lessons. Take a look at a sampling of some of my log entries: 04/04/43 – 30 minutes, 04/09/43 – 36 minutes, 04/24/43 – 37 minutes. You get the idea. It took me 8 hours and 53 minutes to solo, over a 5-month period. I couldn't afford to do any better. To this day, I still cherish and log every minute of my flying time and will even stoop over to pick up a penny if I spot one on the ground. To their everlasting credit, Buck's seaplane employees never complained about launching their J3 Cubs for such short duration flights. I am in awe of how much they assisted this young aviator. I doubt that anyone in business would put up with this today. That is a real shame. The people I knew in aviation during those days were never in it for money, but for the sheer delight of becoming detached from earthly things on a regular basis and sharing their skills with others. My on again/off again schedule continued until I soloed on September 28, 1943 in J3 Cub N41247, just 14 days after my 16th birthday.

It was customary to buy ones flight instructor a pint of booze, then present it in person on that special day. The booty was accumulated and hidden away, until there were enough pints of the stuff to throw a "solo party" at the base. Shopping for the cheapest brand, I was too young to partake in the sampling of this whiskey, but those of legal age never seemed to complain about the booze quality, probably because it was free!

What Aviator can ever forget that day…the day on which they first soloed?

"THAT DAY"

*"That Day", alone I slipped those bonds of Earth
Free – to ride unseen waves on high with new found thoughts
I didn't even know existed.
Hushed – save the murmur of the wind nudging and playing
over and around.
Bits of metal and wood and cloth – molded into a thing of grace.
A gossamer form, we became one – neither the master.
Why was I there – what element of fate allowed me that special
experience?
To reason is fruitless, so I'll not try.
Again and again my thoughts go aloft. I relive those moments,
clearly absorbing the view.
Of mountain peaks, snow capped so small below.
Contrails from other man made machines... wonder if they feel
like me?
Descent we must and we do – embraced again – by routine
things. But:
Call me never again earthman, for I've experienced flight
for the sake of flight alone – yes,
I've been able to touch the hand of God, in a special way.
Realist that I am, I continue with earth bound chores,
knowing full well that
The feelings I have are limited to just a few.
I'll soar again, among invisible forces. For each time I do,
new things are learned about myself – things I never knew.
Airmen have hinted these things and it mattered little.
Now though, it has me entrapped with full knowledge that
Fly again I must... indeed I will.
You know my feeling fellow airmen, for there's little doubt, you
too
Have never forgotten – "That Day".*

By: Author

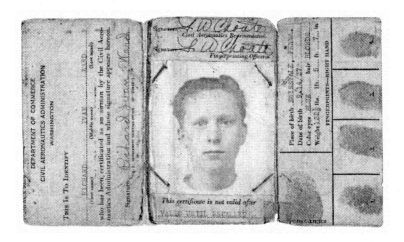

MY FIRST PILOT LICENSE IDENTIFICATION – 1943
R. Ward Collection

In my thoughts, I still ponder over the quality of flight instruction, then and now. Little doubt exists that our generation was awarded the legacy of flight in more of a seat of the pants way, and some of those skills probably saved me from my own stupidity through the years. But on the other hand, I think the professional flight instructors today provide more of a technical base for the students that is much more thorough in detail. You hear the term he/she is a "good stick". A title bestowed upon one by other pilots, this endearment certainly must be earned, then or now. Here is a small personal example of what I think of by the term "seat of the pants." My instructor, the one who soloed me on "That Day," Virginia Givens, was a good-looking gal. The guys not only admired her flying skills, but…. Well, you know what I mean!

On August 7, 1944, my logbook shows an entry just 10 hours and 24 minutes after my first solo. In the remarks column, I noted "Forced Landing – engine cut out in glide".… Unstated in that log entry is that the propeller stopped rotating while exiting the backside of a loop. This occurred over Pittsburgh's North Side, somewhere around my Aunt Betty's house where we lived on Evergreen road. Doing a loop in a J3 Cub seaplane has little bearing on the story in reality. It took very little urging of the instructor by any student to add a few loops during our primary training. Hell! Everyone liked to do them. What is significant is that the engine quit and the river was a 'fer piece' away toward the horizon. I felt seaplanes were to be landed on water, so that's where I headed. Getting to that body of water to this day seemed like a lifetime. Someone was watching over me, because I was able to stretch that glide far enough to fly about 50 feet over the walls of the state penitentiary, located on the shore of the Ohio River, where I slid in for a perfect dead stick landing. Moments later a boat from the penitentiary came roaring out to me, as I floated midstream along with the river current. The folks on board the boat were pleasant enough, but you can only imagine the thoughts that ran through my mind after violating the air rule of never flying low over a prison. After explaining what happened, they lashed a line from their launch onto a cleat on the float of N41554 and offered to tow me back several miles to the seaplane base. I decided to first step out on the starboard float and see if I could get the engine started. With a couple of hand pulls of the prop from the rear, the engine roared to life and my newfound friends from the penitentiary cast off the line. Did I fly back to the base? Certainly not! But I did go back all the way in a high-speed taxi on the step of the floats. All of this leads up the real message behind this story. When I got back to the base and explained to Al Buck what had occurred, the first question out of his mouth was – "Did you pull out the carburetor heat? It's a fine day for icing." My comment back to him was – "The carburetor what?" You guessed it! Virginia had never explained this particular push-pull control to me. I later discovered that I was not alone. A couple of other pre-solo students, when queried, admitted the same thing. I have reflected on this experience time and time again, and I think I know why this void in her training occurred. Understand that the early J3 Cubs were soloed for weight and balance reasons from the back seat; therefore the instructor rode in the front. The carburetor heat push-pull lever on this particular model was mounted low on the right side of the front seat, on the cabin wall, so as to be accessible to both pilots. Hardly any dimensional clearance existed between Virginia's fine looking *derriere*, and the push-pull lever. My guess is that she knew quite well about the use of carburetor heat and simply manipulated it herself. Upon reflection, there is no way that I could have pulled and pushed this control without brushing, if not actually getting, a good feel of Virginia's behind. That's what immediately comes to mind, when I hear the expression "seat of the pants flying." It sure makes one wonder about the quality of flight instruction – then and now. Don't think I am not acutely aware of carburetor icing conditions, to this day. Virtually all of the primary student pilots I have trained through the years have heard this true story. My guess is that none of them have ever forgotten to pull on Carburetor Heat.

Having then received all of my hours in seaplanes by accumulating 14 hours and 32 minutes, I decided to travel to Conway Airport near Baden, PA and checkout in an airplane with wheels. This field had a very short grass runway, but with my instructor sitting in front of me in Piper J3 - NC28089, I succeeded in greasing the machine on the sod during the first landing. My instructor, who's name was Buck Allen, according to my log book, must have been so impressed that he got out of the airplane and sent me on my way. Then, after four.... count them...four solo approaches, I was finally able to establish the glide in such a manner that I put the darned thing down on the ground without scratching it. After all, I had been flying on the river with an unlimited runway length, so the holding of a precise airspeed on final approach to get into short fields was not a major factor in my training. I guess Buck Allen thought I was simply practicing, because he never came up to me after the flight to suggest that I receive some more dual. It did not seem to matter to me either, since I hardly had enough money to pay him for his first 12 minutes. Do you see what I mean about the quality of instruction in those days?

WHY MUST I FLY!

When I fly, the corners of my mind views much more than the instruments ahead.
Pilots know these feelings, though our words are rarely said.
Ever lie on the ground watching night's star-soaked sky,
Absorbing its limitless view?
Or stroll along in the fresh country snow,
Painting thoughts you alone only know?

Ever eat your lunch way up high in a tree . . . Watch a face
in the clouds only you can see?
S'pose you've never shared your thoughts with a dove or a gull .
. .
None of these things?
Then I'm sorry for you, for then you could clearly see a part of
yourself,
A part you never knew.

Why must I fly? The answer lies here

By: Author

ONE OF PITTSBURGH'S MANY SEAPLANE BASES
CIRCA 1940'S
J. Graham Collection

When not thinking of flying, recreation almost always involved making the circuit of Pittsburgh's various roller skating rinks with primary focus on Pittsburgh's famous West View Park. The Waltz,

Tango, you name it, I could do them all at that time, and in my mind can still do them with the grace they deserve, except, I don't think I'll take the risk. That's where I originally met Donna before I went into the Navy Air Corps, while working as a guard on the roller rink floor. She was a child model who's Mother and Father were also divorced. Her Mom died much too young, resulting in her being raised by her very strict "Gram O'Leary". It was my assumption that the only reason Gram allowed me to be around her beautiful granddaughter was because she somehow got the idea that I was part of Pittsburgh's wealthy Ward Baking Company family. Far be it for me to spoil her thoughts. It was easy to perpetuate the myth by simply keeping my mouth shut. I had no idea at the time how it happened, but it seemed that Gram finally leaned toward me, in spite of the many other guys courting Donna, possessing social and financial status far beyond that which I thought could ever be mine.

Shortly after WWII ended and I was discharged from the Navy Air Corps, I took Donna on her first official date. It was an airplane ride in my newly acquired military surplus Fairchild PT19. I could never understand how Gram ever permitted this event to occur, but I found a clue after she passed away. While rummaging through some old pictures, sure enough, there was a picture of her with an unidentified friend standing beside what appears to be a Curtis seaplane (Circa 1910). Having been born in 1890, she must have been about 20 years old then. The truth then became obvious. Gram liked airplanes, and for that I thank the good Lord, since it probably gave me a competitive leg up against Donna's other boyfriends.

In the end though, victory was mine. Eventually, on November 19th 1949, Donna became my lifetime partner, friend and lover. Gram finally learned the real truth about the real Dick Ward. I hardly had a penny to my name save the little asset I had in my flying machine. In the years following our marriage and preceding her passing on, Gram and I became really good friends; I think she loved me even more when I finally became successful in business. Just kidding Gram! Our marriage of over 54 years has resulted in more challenges and fun than any two people deserve. Our three boys and their families are our absolute delight. It shall not pass without my telling you another major key to our successful marriage.

During our engagement, while on the dance floor, Donna whispered, "If it were to be between me and airplanes, which would it be?" I responded – "Donna- you should never ask that question!" …She never has! Being a singer extraordinaire Donna's passion then and to this date is music. Would I ever query her as to a what-if choice? No way! I might hear something that I would not like to hear.

Whatever set of circumstances molded my being in those early years is beyond my mental grasp. Though complex, one fact seems clear in my mind. Not only did I pursue my love for aviation, but also equally important, those around me permitted this to happen. I cringe at the thought that all of this might have been different.

GRAM O'LEARY (RIGHT) ON SEAPLANE
CIRCA 1910
Photographer unknown

CHAPTER III
THE NAVY YEARS

AFTER THE JAPANESE ATTACK on Pearl Harbor, there simply was no question about it in my mind. I was destined to enroll in the military and go off to war and fight the bad guys just as soon as our government would have me. First I enrolled in the Army A6 Pilot Cadet program and went through all of the tests, physical etc, and even got sworn in. Shortly thereafter, I received a letter from the war department telling me that the quota for army pilots was full at the time and that I could go into the Air Corps to become a bombardier, navigator, or as an option take an honorable discharge. I took the discharge and promptly sidestepped to the Navy Air Corps and enlisted. Rather than wait for the pilot openings, I had a chance to go in as a Combat Air-Crew Flight Engineer and decided to grab it, considering my young experiences already acquired as an aircraft mechanic. In retrospect, this was one of the best decisions of my life, since it provided me with a base for my future career in aviation. Of course, at the time, this was not planned, except by destiny.

Boot camp was fought at the "Battle of Millington;" a Naval Base located near Memphis, Tennessee. If you were in the military, you may agree that the "boot" experience will forever be imprinted upon your mind. I believe it serves me well to this day. The shaving of our heads, severe discipline, involvement with Naval traditions and our platoon marching to the tune of "Sky Anchors Away," for this budding aviator it made me proud to be serving our nation in time of war. I still love to march. Ask our three boys! They were each taught the technique when we took walks around the neighborhood, as I called cadence. "Your left...your right...your left right left. I left my wife and forty-eight kids, an old gray mare and a peanut stand... your left... your right... your left.".

After graduation day, there was an indulgence of generous quantities of very low octane beer they served we "Airedales", at a local downtown bar named "Daisy May's"... I marvel at how I am able to remember seemingly unimportant things like the name of that bar, when I can hardly remember my next-door neighbor's name. It is my theory that in later years, ones mental "hard drive" becomes so full of trivialities that at some point, there is little room for more important information to enter. Could that possibly be? If there were just some way of dumping old useless data from ones mind and permitting new things to enter, we'd all be better off. Hell, why not. This system works quite well on our real computer hard drives, and a fortune lies in front of the person who develops the process! Maybe I'll work on that idea!

Shipping out to the next 'Battlefield', our class traveled by troop train directly to the Navy Mechanic School in Norman, Oklahoma, then on to Naval Air Station Cecil Field, in Jacksonville, Florida, for our Gunnery training. This all lead to my assignment to serve with squadron VPB-204 as a Flight Engineer on Martin PBM-5's in Panama's Coco Solo Naval Air Station for the duration. Anti-submarine patrol and air-sea rescue were our missions, with average flights of well over 5 hours. Many lasted over 8 hours, with missions all the way to Bermuda. Circling the fleet in an air-sea rescue mode while they were in operation was called "Dumbo." These flights could last a long time but the boredom was occasionally broken up by one of the carrier guys tucking his Corsair propeller between our float and the hull, while flying in formation. What a sight. Unfortunately, I did not own a camera to record these moments of excitement. From the launching of PBM to the delightful sound of those 2,000 HP engines, and the occasional jet assisted take-offs, to "making the buoy" and beaching our machine. It was all an experience, never to be forgotten.

MARTIN PBM PATROL BOMBER
R. Ward Collection

The PBM was a slow but powerful pure seaplane twin-engine patrol bomber, carrying a crew of seven. Manufactured by Martin and powered with a pair of Pratt & Whitney R2800 engines, it grossed out at 56,000 pounds. It carried twin 50 caliber turrets in the nose, amidships and tail, as well as two bomb bays. Submarine hunting was done visually, as well as with radar and the use of radio sonobuoys. These small radios were dropped in patterns around a suspected area and the radio signals triangulated to determine the position of a submarine. Nothing in flight happened very fast with this historic aircraft but we did have bunks and a full galley aboard. Flight food rations were exceptional, except for the rather bitter "Donald Duck" brand orange juice. Then there was the "raisin bread." Raisin bread became commonplace for the following reason, as reported directly to me from one of the Mess Cooks. He said that it was virtually impossible to eliminate the weevils from the flour used in baking. These little black critters apparently loved the tropical climate environment. It was an annoyance for all of us, but picking the weevils out of the white bread was part of the eating ritual. Sure, the sailors complained but we picked out the weevils and ate the bread anyhow. The problem was almost resolved when they started placing more and more raisins in the bread. The weevils seemed to meld into the overall piece of bread, but the raisins were larger than the weevils and you still had to pick them out. The solution? Grind up the raisins! That ended the problem. The weevils were finally nowhere to be seen. Our ordinance-man was generally in charge of the galley when on patrol in our PBM. We never complained about his cooking, otherwise this duty might be passed along to the complainer. Speaking of chow! Who ever having served at the "Gitmo" Navy base on the island of Cuba can forget the great food? My memory seems to recall that their cooking won many Navy fleet awards.

Our seaplane ramp sat directly under and alongside a cliff leading up to the main airfield. Being quite isolated from the rest of the base, we were able to mill around in anything from dungarees and T-shirt to just a pair of navy boxer shorts. I recall one day, when some officer from the base brought a Wave officer down on the ramp and she got all bent out of shape at the sight of so many men out of uniform. To his credit, I heard her escort say to her – "Just what the hell do you expect? You asked to come down here to men's country and now you want to complain?" That ended that! She probably had dreams that night of what was under all of our shorts.

PBM Operations taught me a lot. The launching and beaching of one of these flying boats was a thing to behold, as was operating at sea from a seaplane tender. These great experiences are imprinted and etched in my mind. Since the PBM was a pure seaplane, except for a very limited number of PBM-5A amphibian versions, they were not easily stored. Most were 'deep six'd' by the Navy. A few made it into the civilian world for use by an array of adventurous opportunists, but water operations were difficult without the proper manpower and beaching equipment. Unfortunately there are literally none left, save a single later model PBM-5A that is now being restored. What a terrible shame! This machine performed its duty in a magnificent manner, but the forthcoming generations will not appreciate its rich history as they might with our other war birds.

To say that I was proud to be a part of this historic squadron is a gross understatement. Being able to finally apply our training in things of the real military aviation world provided this young airman with a sense of accomplishment, valued to this day.

The designer of the VPB-204 Insignia shown on the bracelet that I wore throughout my Navy tour had this to say about his work. "The squadron insignia is one in which all members of the squadron can take pride. It tells a story, in itself, much better than could be told in words. It points out the past endeavors and future aims of the squadron; it stands for some of the individuals and yet gives a picture of the whole; it tells a part of the story of the war against submarines and the squadron's place in this type of warfare."

"The Indian has long been a symbol of America. He has always been thought of as a crafty hunter and a foe to reckon with. And so the Indian head was chosen as being symbolic of the squadron, peering over a cloud stalking his prey, the submarine. But the insignia tells more than that. The Indian is a hunter and as such he must have fitting equipment to supplement his natural talents. He is a warrior, thus he must have adequate weapons with which to combat his enemies. Therefore, our symbolic Indian is seen holding a lantern to hunt down the foe and a flat nose depth bomb to destroy his enemy.

The touch of red on his war plume is a constant reminder to those who are familiar with the meaning of the insignia, that members of the squadron have lost their lives in action. On his headband can be found the victory "V" both in code and lettering."

SQUADRON VP 204 BRACELET INSIGNIA & COMBAT
AIRCREW WINGS
R. Ward Collection

I think of so many things that made life interesting during my VPB-204 tour in Panama. Not all of them relate to flying. Among many, the following two incidents are impregnated in the crevasses of my mind. They both relate to "breaking points".

Some detached duty would move our flight operations from Coco Solo NAS to the NAS Guantanamo Bay in Cuba, better known as Gitmo. During one of these tours, myself along with a couple of my inseparable aircrew mates, namely Dick Bland, a Flight Engineer, and "Woody" Woodruff, an Aircrew Ordinance man, decided to make a beer run across the bay to frequent the infamous bars at Caimanera. These two guys accompanied me throughout my Navy tour, and were simply fun to be around. No one who sampled Cuba's famous and powerful "Chief Hatuey" Beer will ever forget the colorful picture of the old Yaino Indian printed on the label of each bottle. Chief Hatuey was involved in some Spanish rebellions during the early 16th century. His name, in fact his rebellion, continues to live on even today, through the distribution of his high-octane brew in certain parts of the world!

Bland was a jovial individual who enjoyed throwing verbal and sometimes abrasive darts toward anyone with whom he associated. It was just his way! We all took it in stride and had just as much fun thrusting our verbal attacks back at him. Where it went wrong that day, I'll never know, but for some reason while the three of us sat around a small table in a cramped and humid Caimanera Bar, Bland was laying it on to Woody hot and heavy, when apparently the breaking point was reached. Woody picked up his beer bottle and stated in very clear terms - "Bland, one more word out of you and the "Chief" will kiss your head!" You guessed it! Bland kept it up and indeed the "Chief" kissed his head! The only salvation was that the bottle must have been made from cheap glass or else Bland's head was extremely hard. Glass flew everywhere. For reasons I don't understand, Bland was able to get on his feet while uttering the following words; "Woody, you'll never hear another word from me." With that, he strolled out of the bar and down the dirt street to wait for the Navy boat to take us back to our seaplane ramp at Gitmo. Bland indeed kept his word. From that date on until we were discharged, the two of them never spoke, unless they were flight crewing on the same PBM. I remained very good friends with both, but on an individual basis.

I was never able to track these two Guys down after the War, though I have tried. Dick Bland was from Faribault, Minnesota. A few years ago, I made contact with his old high school class reunion chairperson. She determined that he was deceased. Woody came from New York. If anyone reading this knows his whereabouts, I would like to hear from him. It sure would be fun to look him up and buy him a case of Chief Hatuey beer. I sure as hell won't "bug" him though.

On a more humorous but ultimately sad note, I share the following incident. It happened at the mess hall at Coco Solo NAS, Panama. Though I vividly do recall the name of the Aircrewman involved, I am going to change the name, since I don't know his whereabouts at this time, nor even if he is still with us. We'll call him "Harris".

It was while standing in a long line for chow at the base mess hall. Lines were never fun, but if you wanted to eat, you stood in line. It was as simple as that. To this day, I refuse to stand in line at a restaurant, and my wife does not quite understand why. My recollection about this particular scene is that I was in line for about 15 minutes and had worked my way to within 5 or so feet from the table where I would pick up my metal tray and pick up my chow. Standing directly in front of me was "Harris." Literally, when Harris was ready to pick up his tray, the Officer of the Day (OD), with his Officer's cap tucked under his left arm, walked directly in front of Harris, scooped up a tray and proceeded to sample the food. This of course was part of the daily duty of the "OD." Well! That action did not agree with Harris whatsoever. In an obvious fit of rage, Harris spouted out in a loud and clear manner...*Sir! If you're so God Damn Hungry, why don't you eat the scrambled eggs on your hat!* The OD, without saying a word, continued in a gentlemanly manner through the chow line, sat down, ate an abbreviated meal and departed without a word to anyone. I sure wish I could remember who that OD was. Perhaps he'll read this and make himself known to me.

Before continuing, you should know that Harris was somewhat different. He was a loner, very skinny and his head resembled that of a skeleton. As I recall, he had very few associates, though frankly, he was always very friendly toward me and I reciprocated during any of our brief encounters. One thing seemed to be very noticeable however; he was constantly being ridiculed by a lot of the other guys over his looks. We've probably all seen this action occur during our travel down life's path. Pick on the weak one in an effort to give one's self strength could be the theory. Have you ever seen a bunch of chickens' gang up on another of their kind? I have! One chicken will peck at the neck of another chicken. Soon another will peck at the same spot. Then another will peck, and on and on until all of the chickens draw blood. All of this directed toward the weak chicken. In retrospect, the whole thing reminds me of the incident with Harris. Perhaps a "shrink" would prove me wrong, but I'm convinced to this day that his frontal attack on the OD, that day in the chow line was the result induced by the action of many of the other men pecking on the weak "chicken" over a period of time. Shortly after the incident Harris was eliminated from the squadron roster of VPB-204 and shipped back to the States. There seemed to be little doubt in anyone's mind that he received a Section 8 discharge.

The story however, does not quite end here. In 1952 I started my own Aircraft Fixed Base Flight & Maintenance Operation in Three Rivers, Michigan, where we still reside. Having purchased N79276, a Cessna UC78 Bamboo Bomber on the Military surplus market for about $600.00, I rebuilt and configured it for my charter airplane. On this particular day, in 1952, I was hired to make an overnight trip to Detroit City Airport. After dropping off my passengers and securing the aircraft, I went outside of the old terminal building and hailed a cab to take me to a downtown hotel. As I entered the cab, I could not believe my eyes. The driver was none other than Harris! Thinking that he would recognize me, I offered a friendly hand toward him, only to discover that he apparently did not recognize me. I voiced something like...."Isn't your name Harris?" When he acknowledged that he was, I reminded him that we were in the same squadron in Panama. His comment was..."I don't remember too much about those days." How very sad, but isn't it human nature to allow painful experiences to fade? How very fortunate many of us are that we can still clearly remember many of those military days as we continue our approach down life's glide path.

Our current family magic carpet is a Beechcraft Model D50 Excalibur conversion model D50C. This model sports a pair of Lycoming IO720 400 HP engines. Having owned a "Twin Bonanza" since 1977, this fantastic flying machine has taken us to many parts of the world, especially in the Caribbean. In February 1986, we embarked on an interesting trip with stops at the Turks and Cacos, San Juan Puerto Rico, Curacao, Panama, Costa Rica, and back to Three Rivers. The stop at Panama was motivated by my desire to retrace the footsteps of my youthful Naval Airman days. To some extent, this could have been a mistake, because nothing is ever as one imagines it to be, after that many years. Perhaps one should not tamper with memories of this sort. I just don't know! On the other hand, I'm glad to have accomplished the visit for a number of reasons, among which includes staying at the historical George Washington Hotel in Colon. While operating out of Coco Solo NAS in Colon Panama, I was always in awe when I looked at this structure, which of course was off limits to the likes of us. This hotel was constructed during the construction of the Panama

Canal and looks directly toward the Atlantic side of its entrance. The majesty of the building was shrouded in a cloud of neglect, but I was able to sense the rich history in a real way, while walking the halls. Naturally, the highlight of that trip was for me, accompanied by Donna, to set foot on the old seaplane ramp. Taking a cab, with a very friendly Panamanian driver, we set out to the old abandoned base. I was not prepared for the emotion that I experienced in a very odd way. It was like walking in another person's shoes as I strolled along the ramps, which were so active in those early years in the 40's. The old derelict tower was still there and even a few parts of the old radio equipment, but the maintenance hangars were completely gone, save the metal door tracks, still attached to the concrete. One of the buoys was sitting by the launching ramp and I stood there like some nut case, trying to hide my tears from Donna, while I touched it, in an effort to refresh my soul. How very small the whole placed looked. It was hard to conceive just how many huge PBM Mariners sat on that seemingly small ramp. The barracks were turned into a school, which unfortunately was locked up over the weekend. I would have enjoyed seeking out the spot where I bunked down. Perhaps I could have spotted a glimpse of the ghost of the guy who used to go around the barracks almost every evening with an electric toaster, loaves of bread and some cheese. Order up a snack and he'd provide a toasted cheese sandwich on demand, for a price of course. This enterprising young airman was looked upon as some sort of a weird loaner. His prime off-hours activity was running an enterprising business hustling toasted cheese sandwiches around the barracks. Why would any red-blooded American airman not take advantage of the great sights and sounds of such places as the Copacabana nightclub in Colon? At my current stage of my life, it's easy to see who the dummy was. That guy, who's name slips my mind, has got to be the retired president of some multi-national Corporation, sitting on his 75 foot yacht, while someone else brings him a toasted cheese sandwich and a beer. All in all, I like to think that VPB-204 helped develop some pretty good aviators and individuals with honorable character. The latter being a trait, it seems to me, which may be more difficult to find these days.

CHAPTER IV
AFTER THE WAR

IT WAS BACK TO PITTSBURGH where my room was still available at Aunt Betty and Uncle Dick's home. Memory recalls that I didn't even ask if it was ok to do so. I guess I just assumed that they were my family and it would be OK. My Mom was still living there so in my mind it was the thing to do. Today, I think times have changed. For good or bad, the extended family has now become the contracted family.

My Navy mustering out pay was disposed of in short order. The day after arriving home my friend "Biggs" outlined a master plan to go in partnership and purchase NC59200, a surplus WWII Fairchild PT19 from the government war assets division. Virtually every make of aircraft was priced something around $600.00 to $800.00. We selected one from the line, and parked the aircraft at Pittsburgh's old Bettis Airport. Biggs, the head truck mechanic at Harmony Dairy Company was as skilled and hardworking as they come. He had a knack for cutting deals with his boss and owner of the company, namely Jim Thompson. On the premise that the PT19 become Harmony's "Company" aircraft, Jim allowed Bob to charge our gas on the Harmony Dairy Gulf Oil Company credit card. I could count the times on one hand that a "Company" trip was ever made for Harmony Dairy, but we sure as heck logged some interesting and valuable flight time. Looking at this in perspective, this was probably Jim's way of showing Biggs some appreciation as an employee... In a manner not realized Jim played a role in developing my own flying skills. Hells bells, there was no way that I could have afforded to pump gas into the old PT19 in those days, other than for an occasional flight. To spend my mustering out pay for this aircraft made no business sense whatsoever, but as it turned out, this was one link on the chain of events that pulled further toward a rewarding and successful life.

Biggs and I liked to fly together, taking turns as pilot in command. It was common for us to plan on going somewhere by looking to see which way the wind was blowing, then cruise cross-county with the wind on our tail with the hopes that it would reverse direction or subside on the return flight. We did that on a flight from Pittsburgh to Harrisburg, then on to Washington DC's National Airport. According to my pilot logbook this was on a weekend in early March of 1948. The many layers of clothing worn made those frosty winter flights slightly bearable. A tad of heat trickled into the front cockpit, but the guy riding in back also retained an old cotton blanket as part of his flight gear, to fend off thermal degradation. At our young ages – coupled with the sheer delight of flight itself, personal comforts were low on the totem pole. Our plan was to return on Sunday, since I had to return to my class at the Pittsburgh Institute Of Aeronautics, where I was then attending school. It was there that I received my Aircraft & Engine Mechanic and A&E Mechanic Instructor ratings. The tailwind heading southeast was moderate, but unfortunately the wind on the return trip was more than a casual breeze. We discovered along the way, that the Gulf Oil Company credit card controlled by Biggs could not be utilized during the re-fueling process, so we dipped into our almost empty pockets to purchase some fuel. The quantity we purchased slips my mind but it related more to our available cash than to the needs of our Fairchild. Nevertheless, we figured we could make the return trip with the fuel we placed on board. That however would not be the case. Tuned to and navigating the low frequency Red 20 low frequency Range, with myself at the controls in the front cockpit and Biggs wrapped up like a cocoon in the rear, it became reality to me that the existing headwind would not permit flying the rest of the way home. The visibility over the hill country was hazy but my fairly precise navigation on the low frequency beam placed me somewhere southeast of Somerset, Pennsylvania. I made an attempt to locate the small landing field and put down at Somerset, but after expanding my search in that remote area and the needles on the wing fuel gauges showing near empty, I decided to find a field and land. Running out of gas was not an option for this airman. While over the little town of Berlin, Pennsylvania (Population about 1,500) I did exactly that. I found a suitable pasture and landed! The aircraft rolled a very short distance accumulating huge globs of mud on the outer rim of the tires and under the wing panels. This was not a happy sight. A gentleman in rubber boots and a pair of overalls wallowed through the mud to see what the hell was going on. He introduced himself as George Dively, the Burgess of the town of Berlin. We had just put down in his back yard! The result was not what you probably expect. We explained that we wanted to leave in the morning, hopefully when the ground became frozen overnight, that we had no money but would like to make contact and ask my Mother to wire some money via Western Union. The care provided to these aviators by Mr. Dively and his family was indeed fortunate and appreciated. He went back to his home, brought out a tractor and dragged our aircraft up to slightly higher ground for the night. He then took us to his home, and told us that his wife was going to give us a home cooked meal. A Western Union telegram was sent off explaining the situation. Donna, my girlfriend (now my wife), got a call from my Mother explaining that I was breaking the date we had planned for Sunday evening. Mom wired the money that arrived the next morning. Off we went to the local automobile filling station and after filling up some five gallon cans several times for the PT19, we took off from Mr. Dively's partially frozen field and headed for Pittsburgh. Many years later, Biggs, while visiting me at our lake home in Three Rivers handed me a small newspaper clipping dated March 7, 1948 that apparently was sent to him by Mr. Dively.

"PLANE MAKES FORCED LANDING IN BERLIN FIELD

Believing themselves near Somerset and being low on fuel two Pittsburgh airmen, Richard Ward and Robert Biggs, made a forced landing safely in Berlin, Sunday at 6 pm. The young men left Pittsburgh Saturday, went on to Harrisburg, then to Washington and were on their way back to Pittsburgh when their gasoline supply got low. Circling around the open field back of Berlin's Burgess George S. Dively's home, they landed safe and sound without damage to the plane, but cold and hungry. Finding the airmen practically in his back yard, the Burgess Dively invited them to supper. Afterwards they went to a hotel and telegraphed home for money that was becoming as low as their fuel, of which there were only four gallons remaining. The landing was somewhat muddy out near the potato chip factory. The pilot, Ward, had been seeking the Somerset airport. If the ground is hard enough today, Monday, to take off, the young men will return to Pittsburgh."

Living on the edge from time to time is a very good thing! It adds spice to an otherwise dull life, but we must always remind ourselves to keep a rope lashed around our waist!

OUR FIRST DATE – DONNA WILSON BY OUR PT19 N95200
Photo By Author

You may have never heard of this school, but I owe a lot to the Pittsburgh Institute of Aeronautics (PIA). There I was able to attend this school using my WWII GI Bill, a government program aimed at transitioning returning war veterans into the civilian workforce. Over an 18-month period, it provided me with a base of knowledge that urged me to fine-tune skills I did not even know existed within my capacity as an individual. I graduated with both a Civil Aeronautics Administration (CAA) approved Aircraft & Engine Mechanic and Aircraft & Engine Mechanic Instructors certificates. Those hands-on mechanical experiences coupled with classroom theory provided me with a 3rd dimension I would have otherwise never had available while developing my business in years that follows. The instructional skills of Arthur Henze, who presided over my very first class, taught me the fine art of working with mercerized cotton and airplane dope to recover the airframes of fabric covered airplanes. It served me well through the years and enabled me to work with this art form not only to make money, but also to restore some of the classic aircraft that I have subsequently owned. The school was and continues to be owned by Jack Graham. During my time a very competent President, Jim Fisher, ran it. Believe me, none of these guys worked for money as their primary goal. Do they make people like this any more? I hope so, but I'm not too sure. For anyone planning to make aviation their career, whether it is engineering, mechanical or even as a pilot, consider adding this mechanical knowledge to your skills portfolio. This fine school still exists today in a well-run facility at the Allegheny County Airport. Our number three Son Greg attended PIA after his tour in Naval Aviation, and is now the Senior Curator of Aircraft Restoration for the Kalamazoo Aviation History Museum (AirZoo) in Kalamazoo, Michigan, doing exotic restorations on rare flying machines. I'm proud to say that in 1968 I received one of the first Distinguished Alumni Awards from PIA. Jim Fisher personally delivered it to me at my home in Michigan, where it is proudly displayed on my office wall to this day.

Post WWII aviation jobs were few and far between, but along the way while attending PIA I met a lifelong friend – Harold Hinton. Harold was married to his childhood friend Violet who still communicates with us from her home in California after Harold's eventual death. Harold retired from McDonnell Douglas as an instructor and head of Flight Engineer training.

During our classes at school, Harold and I always teamed up together and provided each other with a large ration of moral support. While other guys were telling each other how rough things were on the job market, we both pushed to the head of the pack in our successful attempts to secure work. Persistence paid off and within a few weeks after graduation, we were both hired at the Curtis-Wright Company in Columbus, Ohio. Curtis-Wright constructed the C46 cargo aircraft for the Army Air Corps. The C46 was originated as a CW20 airliner with the prototype flying in

1940. It was presumed that it could compete with the DC3, but with the upcoming Second World War, the US Army placed an order for 40 of these unpressurized cargo versions and in July of 1942, the first of 3,182 aircraft deliveries started. Its primary fame in military use was flying cargo on the "The Hump" route over the Himalayas between India and China. When world peace finally came, it was discovered that these surplus airplanes could then be used in the commercial freighter marketplace. The tough airframe made it a popular machine for this purpose.

Being hired in at Curtis-Wright to work as a mechanic on fuel system upgrades during the complete overhaul of the airframe and engines, provided hands on experience. It became personally rewarding, as was my meager weekly paycheck.

Things were serious between Donna, now my fiancée working as a Legal Librarian in Pittsburgh and myself, so this distance became an inconvenience, to say the least. But the lesson here was that you went where the work was. Violet moved to Columbus with Harold and to my good fortune, they were able to secure an apartment in the same building where I rented a single sleeping room. To their everlasting credit, they shared their dinners with me every day. Violet could make a banquet out of almost anything and it was always good. My meager financial donation to the food kitty was always welcome. They were lean years, but again, no one ever told us that we were poor. Life was good!

Cars were very expensive after the war, but I was somehow able to swing the purchase of an old overpriced Dodge Coupe. Using a spray attachment from an Electrolux vacuum sweeper, I gave it a red paint job that ended up looking like a Venetian blind going down the road, because I had to thin down the paint enough to make it go through that cheap sprayer. Pride of ownership of a car was low on my priority list, so that's how it stayed until it fell apart from other mechanical wear and tear. I was at least thankful that it got me back and forth to be with my sweetheart Donna on the weekends. That 3½-hour trip from Columbus to Pittsburgh started at midnight, since I worked the nightshift at Curtis-Wright. With hardly anyone on the road, the white center line had a hypnotic effect that I will never forget. I ashamedly admit I have horrid memories of going down the highway shutting one eye, then the other, as though this did any good. If I did shut both eyes at once in a resting mode, damned if I'll publicly admit it in this forum. Opening the car window and blasting air in my face also seemed to do little more than mess up my hair. Thinking back, I can still remember driving on a dark empty straight length of highway and slamming on the brakes to a skidding stop after seeing a blinking red light flash directly in my windshield. The red light was there OK. But I soon discovered that it was marking a crossroad that proved to be at least a half-mile down the highway. Young and stupid! Does that cover it? Donna was waiting for me!

During my early employment at Curtis-Wright, a union representative approached me. Employment there was based upon the "open shop" principle. If you wanted to pay monthly dues to have someone represent you, it was an option. Conversely, if you wanted to speak for yourself, as did I, you did not have to join the Union. I have no knowledge what the ratio of union to nonunion personnel was but the hardcore Union bosses continually kept bugging me to give them a portion of my hard earned money. Their pitch always came down to the fact that they were going to get more money for me. Nothing was ever said as to what they could do to help the company, which by the way was struggling to get more contracts. I used to tell them what dumb jerks they were and almost came to blows with one of them when they began to talk about striking the company to make it a closed shop. All the while, I could see the last airplane to be overhauled on a government contract sitting on the outside ramp line, with nothing following its tail. Since my Mother did not raise a dummy, I decided to get out while this choice was still an option after being offered a job as an instructor at a small GI Bill aircraft & engine mechanic school in Leechburg, Pennsylvania. True to their word, a short time after I left, with no regard for the well being of the company but rather, only their greed, the Union struck Curtis–Wright. Their management put a lock on the door and closed the plant forever. I felt bad for the company as well as the innocent persons caught up in this stupid move, and it cemented my negative thoughts about labor unions to this very day.

Working at the Leechburg School of Aeronautics provided an opportunity to learn teaching techniques and I was even able to start an aerial advertisement business on the side in partnership with a fellow who owned a surplus Cessna UC78 "Bamboo Bomber". I purchased and installed a set of government surplus University model 4A4 loudspeakers in the baggage compartment. The installation was complete with a huge dynamotor, record machine and turntable. Our plan was to play music to gain attention from the throngs below, before blasting them with our live microphone commercial advertising. Those were the days when loudspeakers were mounted on the roof of an automobile for advertising purposes. Try that today and someone will probably come up and read you your rights. The manager of a drive-in movie heard about my brainstorm and with a small amount of money up front, he became our number one customer. Unfortunately, the systems with all of its power sounded like ocean waves hitting the beach, rather than anything resembling quality commercial advertising. To solve the problem, I mounted an electric wench and with the push of a button on a winch, the set of speakers would lower on a 100- foot cable. The music could now be heard but my voice was not clear. The problem was finally solved when Donna was appointed to do the speaking. The higher pitch of a woman's voice did the trick and we were finally able to earn our modest fee.

November 19, 1949 was my all time date to remember. Donna and I tied our knot in marriage. Our lives were to become one, a reality that continues to this day. What a blessing this has been! Having a partner of her caliber surely fueled the engine of my own success, both as a person and in business. She made it easy for me to navigate uncharted territories and pursue my own activities with virtually no complaining. Lord – can there be another like her in this world? Donna tells me that her own Gram O'Leary passed along this saying: *"The tightest way to hold your husband is to hold him loose."* Gram O'Leary's own success in marriage was an obvious example of some of her wisdom.

To tell a story showcasing the life of Donna Wilson Ward would take a separate book to do justice to her many facetted attributes and activities. It was put well by our seemingly confirmed bachelor, #2 son Mark, when queried about a marriage in his own future. His reply? "I'm still looking for someone like Mom!" Donna's natural and inner beauty, her musical and singing ability and the awesome sensitivity she displays in being able to assist others barely scratches the surface, in an effort to try and describe this beautiful being.

HONEYMOON

A friend loaned this car, powered by a V8 engine to us for our honeymoon. The photographer took this candid picture just as a smoke bomb ignited when the ignition was turned on. The next day on our trip to Tennessee during the first gas stop, the attendant motioned for us to come and look under the hood. A sign placed there by a person or persons unknown stated "Gas Station Attendant – Just married – Pull a spark plug lead"... In addition to the sign, he pointed to one of the spark plug leads that were burned completely in two from the smoke bomb. We had traveled all of that distance on only 7 cylinders. The car ran just fine as far as I was concerned. I had never driven with 8 cylinders before. After a repair, we were on our way.
R. Ward Collection

The modest second story apartment on Kimble Avenue in Arnold Pennsylvania was the first place we called home. Located somewhere between Leechburg and downtown Pittsburgh, where Donna was employed at a large law firm, we were each able to head off to work in different directions. It seems now that our lives were much less cluttered during those early years. Television was not a part of our lives, but the magic of radio gave us mental visions far beyond that which could ever be displayed on the tube. How unfortunate that the current generation missed being a part of that bygone era.

The Mechanic Instructing job at Leechburg Pennsylvania was going well, but I had an opportunity to secure a Chief Instructor job at a school in Martinsburg, West Virginia and took it. The pay differential was hardly worth talking about, but the school was far better equipped for the task. During those days, the GI Bill was a fruitful income generator for those who tailored their business to conform to the voluminous government red tape. The experiences I was able to glean from working in a management capacity for Martinsburg Aircraft Service would serve me well in preparation for the next phase of my career, that of starting my own business. I had no intention of changing positions until it became clear to me that the owners were too used to the revenue wave created from the GI Bill income. I could easily see that the end of the GI Bill was ahead of us so I decided to sell the owners on the idea of making a transition to the civilian marketplace. To put my money where my mouth was, I told them that I would take over the night school for a period of time, in order to release myself for selling the services of our training to the public during the day. There would be no additional charge to the school for my services, not even for gasoline for my car, during the necessary travel. My wish was granted and I traveled from high school to high school in the surrounding cities, giving talks to perspective seniors about the advantages of entering into the world of aviation as a government rated aircraft and engine mechanic. My efforts were rewarded when I was able to sign up and get deposits from fifteen young men for a new class that started immediately after their high school graduation. The owners gave me an "atta-boy", but made no effort whatsoever to continue on with either a recruiting program or funding for the required advertisement to make this transition occur. The reality of the situation hit me like a ton of bricks and I could see that the owners having to go to work to make the conversion from the easy dollar days that the GI bill dragged in was simply not going to happen. With a "Trade-A-Plane" magazine in hand, I started searching the classified ads in an attempt to locate a place to start up a business of our own. This was done in full view of the owners. In fact, one of them was kind enough to allow me the use of his private aircraft to go to Michigan to look over one possibility.

Regarding the fate of Martinsburg Aircraft Service, a number of months after I departed, the school had a mysterious fire and burned to the ground. The theory being passed around was that some highly flammable magnesium shavings around a band saw decided to self ignite in the dark of night. Hmm - Oh sure it did!

CHAPTER V
A TRANSITION INTO BUSINESS

MY EXTREMELY UNDERSTANDING and now pregnant wife Donna didn't complain when I announced we were going to gamble the family fortune of $800.00 by leaving Martinsburg, West Virginia and start our own business. My dreams were about to take flight. In the early 1950's private aviation, as it was called then, was in the doldrums and the forecast of having a post war airplane in every garage did not come about. One thing I knew for certain was that I should control my own destiny and not rely on others. I had a set of hand tools, lots of skills and was willing to work 15-hour days. I noticed while looking over Trade-A-Plane there were a number of small community airports that were up for grabs. The deal generally was that you would be permitted to eek out a living on their airport doing what you could to make some money, if you would provide the community with free managerial services. The title of Airport Manager would carry with it a number of responsibilities beyond that of an "executive position." This would include but not be limited to such mundane things as mowing the grass on the airfield. Zeroing in on one such opportunity in Grand Haven, Michigan, I borrowed my boss' Piper J4 and paid a visit to meet with J. B. Simms, the airport board manager. The feature of this package was that they owned a house on the airport and would allow us to use it free of charge. With a tentative commitment, I returned to Martinsburg only to find a telegram waiting for me from Bob Shumaker, the chairman of the airport board of Three Rivers, Michigan. Just that fast and by some twist of fate, the word had spread that there was a 'live one' out there. The wire pleaded with me not to make a final decision until I met with their airport board. Not having the guts to again ask to use my boss' airplane, I immediately drove to Three Rivers from Martinsburg.

At the time, there were a lot of similarities between these two small communities. The population was about the same and there was a largely populated area within 20 miles from each. The airports themselves were the usual unpaved sod and each had a small terminal building with an oil-burning stove for heat. Both also had a hangar that could be turned into a shop to work on aircraft. In the final analysis and without hesitation, I chose Three Rivers because the location provided a much better climate for winter operations. Grand Haven is directly on the shore of Lake Michigan with its more severe Lake Michigan effect on the weather.

TAKE CONTROL OF YOUR LIFE
ON A MOMENT TO MOMENT BASIS

Somewhere along the line, I discovered I was using a Technique that serves me well. I declared that procrastination is an evil attribute and should never be included in my lifestyle.
The more I observed others procrastinate, the more it became crystal clear that this action has become the rule, rather than the exception, for the majority of those persons whom I have known. How very sad indeed!

By Author

In the spring of 1952, we moved from Martinsburg West Virginia to Three Rivers, Michigan and started our own Fixed Base Operation (FBO) business. Our $800.00 purchased an Aeronca 7AC Champ with a total time of only 700 hours on both the airframe and engine. That was my instructional, rental and charter aircraft at "Ward Aero"... Those were the days when we charged a buck per horsepower to overhaul an engine, plus parts, of course. That's right!

I would overhaul your aircraft engine for a dollar per horsepower plus parts. 65 Horsepower – 65 bucks! The Champ rented for $6.00 per hour solo and $8.00 dual. Charter flights were 17 cents per flying mile. My first shop was in a small T-Hangar with a cinder floor and no heat where I took on the task of painting a Cessna 120 fuselage for $70.00 – parts and labor.

Our reception in the community could not have been better. We were invited to reside with Clark and Clara Belle Jacobs for a few months, until we found a place to stay. Clark was a pillar of the community, a longstanding local flier and a member of the airport board. Instantly, Donna was recruited to the Presbyterian Church choir due to her expert singing skills, where she still sings to this day. I took care of business while Donna unselfishly took care of me. The community embraced her completely to a point where I eventually became known as "Donna's husband." Along the way and after joining our local Rotary Club, I finally became recognized for who I was. That went along fine, until our number 2 son Mark was accepted into the Air Force Academy, and with the town folks being equally proud of this fact, my identity once again became clouded. Then I became known as "Mark's Father." What's a guy to do?

How we made it through those early years is nothing short of a miracle, but I think our success in part had something to do with steadily working 15 hour days, 7 days a week, 52 weeks per year. The company accounting system then consisted of two spindles on the worktable. (No desk!) When a bill came in, it was placed on one spindle. Pay the bill and it was moved to the other. Sometimes the movement was terribly slow. I discovered early in the game that it was proper to pay others what you owed them, before you gave yourself a nickel. The tire inner tube patches Donna placed on my winter rubber boots paid homage to that rule. No one told us that we were poor or as it is now expressed by the politically correct – "below the poverty level." This never even entered our minds. We had each other, the start of a family, supportive friends, and an airplane. Life was good!

With no way to afford employees, it was common practice to leave a note on the door of the airport's small terminal building while I was on a charter trip. The door was left open, so a pilot could call Donna to come to the airport to provide gasoline. Off to the airport 6 miles away she would go with our firstborn son Dane in her arms. Sunup to sundown were the hours. On the bad weather days, and Southwest Michigan has its share of those, when there was no work in the shop, I filled my time constructing an HO gauge railroad layout that I proudly displayed in a small room adjacent to the T-Hangar shop.

Satisfying calls from the public requesting to charter an airplane for trips was initially made possible by my being able to lease a Stinson Voyager from one of the flying clubs on the field. About a year later, I secured a military surplus twin engine Cessna T50 for $600.00 with bad fabric and in need of a center section spar inlay and proceeded to work on this with gusto. About a year and over 55 gallons of Butyrate Dope later, I was able to complete the work and place this in the flying fleet, alongside our Aeronca 7AC trainer. The *Bamboo Bomber*, as it was called in the military, with its two radial Jacobs engines sported a neat gray/blue paint job with a white top. The "executive interior" sported some leather and curtains sewn by Donna. It had a roomy cabin with pilot and copilot seats, plus a large three-place couch in the back. Legroom abounded! The 4 course low frequency radio ranges were still in use throughout the U. S., so the military radio was still useable. However, it also had the very first model of the NARCO Omni receiver installed, which would just occasionally work and only somewhat correctly. It was the first model omni receiver to be introduced to the civilian market and I learned soon enough to revert to the direction finder low frequency loop antenna when the omni receiver failed to operate properly.

CESSNA T50 - "BAMBOO BOMBER" N79276
Circa 1954 R. Ward Collection

During the reconstruction process, I decided to remove the pilot's relief tube since privacy on any charter trip was hardly possible. One day, Dr. John Jacobowitz, an acquaintance with a WWII military pilot background stopped by and asked if I could secure a relief tube for him. Producing the one I had just removed, I presented it to him. I was busy at the time and did not even ask the obvious question. Why did he want this object? That episode was forgotten for over 30 years when it popped into my mind while attending a local Christmas party. The Doctor was there and it struck me that I should now find out the answer to that question. John went on to describe how he had made a small stand for the small funneled object and placed it on the top of his bar. When someone ordered a mixed drink, he would use it to measure the proportions. This small act provided him with surges of glee through the many remaining years of his life. If the person spotted him in the act of mixing the drink and said nothing, he would chuckle to himself, and say nothing. If the person was a pilot, they both got a belly laugh. For him, it was the small things in life that make the difference. How very correct this concept is!

This useful object adorned his bar from the early 1950's until he went west about 50 years later. His widow, Virginia, later desired to appraise some of his military materials to donate to the Kalamazoo Aviation History Museum and eventually called upon me to estimate their values. I did so with one proviso…. I would be able to get back the "Martini Mixer." She knew the story very well and presented this precious artifact to me unceremoniously with a hearty "thanks for the loan." It is now prominently displayed in my hangar office as a tribute to Dr. Jacobowitz' captivating sense of humor.

PICTURE OF MARTINI MIXER
R. Ward Collection

In its day, the Cessna "Bamboo Bomber" generated a huge ration of very interesting charter trips, not the least of which were originated by a wealthy businessman who owned the largest automotive salvage yard in Michigan. Harry Gottlieb, originally from Chicago, was in the automotive salvage business in Three Rivers in a big way. Harry reportedly sipped as much as a fifth a day, but I never did see him staggering drunk. I learned to respect him with all of his faults, though he definitely provided me with some interesting episodes.

The trips with Harry were too numerous to cover in this writing, but I certainly appreciated his business in those start up lean years. A few of them however are positioned permanently in my memory bank. While Harry originated most of the trips he was more or less the spokesman for the group of guys he liked to associate with. Beaver Island Michigan, positioned in Lake Michigan north of Traverse City and west of the Straights of Mackinac was the destination for a huge portion of these trips. With its remote location, rich history of the Mormon King Strang days during the 1850's and especially the Shamrock Inn, it seemed to some to be the place to go.

Typically, I would get a call during the day or at some odd hour of the night with the proclamation that they were ready to go to Beaver Island. "They" meant Harry and others from our surrounding area, such as Kalamazoo. On occasion, Harry would include an extra passenger that he declared was his bodyguard. This gentleman was employed by the Three Rivers Police Department. I silently named the group "the village idiots," but only to myself. On arrival over the Island, I would buzz the small town of St. James, and Bub Burke the driver of the one and only cab would make his trek to the airport and pick us up. Often I stayed at Bub's residence in a small bunkhouse in the rear, but more often I would make my way to the Lighthouse on the south shore and stay in an extra room provided by Johnnie Gallagher the Coast Guard Lighthouse Keeper. Johnnie was a great person who took this young aviator under his wing.

The real destination on Beaver Island was the Shamrock Inn. It still exists today, but I question if the spirit of the establishment can match those earlier days. The cook at the Shamrock would fix up the finest steak dinner one could experience, but first we had to go to the store next door and have some meat sliced off an aging cow's carcass hanging in the cooler at the rear of the store. This job oft times became mine, as part of the pilot ground time for which I was charging. Not that I minded that chore. It enabled me to direct the cutting process, so we all ended up with more than enough to eat. Each time, Harry would remind me to get the steaks from an area on the cow where the mold had to be scraped away, implying that the aging process employed by the butcher would produce a better cut. It absolutely did!

St. Patrick's Day was always worth a trip to Beaver Island, and an evening hanging out at the Shamrock. I did this only one time, but it was enough. Sometime during the not too late hours, the place exploded into a right out of a movie bar room brawl. Bottles and chairs started flying around the room. I positioned myself under one of the tables and retreated to the street at the earliest opportunity. I later learned that this was an annual event that, if memory serves me, was ignited between the French & Irish residents of the Island and some of the Coast Guard guys. The next day, I was told that the fights progressed down the road and ended up at the Coast Guard

Station lighthouse, not too far from town. With no movie in town, presumably one has to be entertained somehow. There was a jail, but I've heard that it was only used once or twice. Holding two people, it consisted of a rectangular structure with open steel straps all riveted together. It sat outside overlooking the harbor within the village. Mysteriously, during the 1930's, it burned and was never replaced. A jail apparently was hardly needed on Beaver Island. Where would one go to escape?

Harry's wife resided in Kalamazoo and was a high-class woman who apparently put up with Harry's odd ways. Donna reminds me of the time that Mrs. Gottlieb called her at our home and explained to her that I should not be flying Harry around, because he would be a bad influence on me. Good try! But it didn't work. For me to drink booze would be self-defeating and I avoided it like the plague. It would be too easy to have to miss a charter trip and the critically needed revenue. Interestingly, Mrs. Gottlieb called our house late one night and asked if I would pick her up in Kalamazoo in the morning and fly to Beaver Island. I assumed that this was an attempt to retrieve her husband. Somehow she knew that I had dropped Harry and several others off the day before. I promptly agreed to do so, explaining that I operated a public charter flying service and would certainly not turn her away. The next morning we made the 225-mile trip, buzzed the town, met Bub, and the hunt began around the island with Bub driving and Mrs. Gottlieb sitting in the back seat. Not wanting to become further involved, I went into a standby mode and went to visit the Coast Guard guys. As Shultz used to say in the TV program Hogan's Heroes, "I know nothing! I see nothing!" After a few hours, I brought Mrs. Gottlieb back, without Harry, who was nowhere to be found on the island. A couple of days later, I picked him up at the Beaver Island airstrip and dropped him off in Kalamazoo.

Our trips to Chicago in the 1950's were always interesting. Harry would reserve rooms at the Lakeshore Hotel. It was an upscale facility far beyond what this poor pilot ever experienced in private life. Harry's attire was, shall we say - casual. Be assured however, when we entered, virtually everyone knew Harry and provided him with the best of service and he returned the complement with a large tip. Once in particular we were picked up by the Chief Detective of the Chicago Police Department, whom Harry had not seen for a number of years. Though I can recall his name, it shall go without repeating here. We spent the day touring the city with emphasis on the Crime Lab at his facility. On the way down the elevator, we were side by side with two mobsters who were shackled. These characters conducted some small talk with Harry's detective friend and after stepping off of the elevator at our floor, he went on to explain that things were changing and not like the old days, where you could simply have a talk with "the boys." I think I knew what he meant. Off the three of us went to a yachting facility to visit another one of their old friends. At the time, he was one of the largest Chris Craft dealers in the USA. Stepping into the owner's office again provided ample opportunity to talk about the good old days, much of which you can probably guess. In an act of confidentiality, Harry requested that I be shown the secret passage out of his office. It was indeed completely hidden and without knowing the location, one could never have found it, let alone the technique to open the door. I entered the tunnel but never went far enough to discover the exit. Ever since I was a kid, I have always wanted my own secret passage, but this was about the nearest I'll ever get to a real one.

The charter flight revenues generated were not all that easy. Occasionally, I got called upon to provide an extra and unexpected service. Take for example the call I received in the early morning hours from one of the hotels in Kalamazoo. Harry wanted to go to Beaver Island but he implied that his gambling buddies would not permit him to leave the room, until he paid off his losses. At his request, I made a run on his behalf to the local Three Rivers bank, was handed several thousand dollars in cash, went up the hotel elevator to the suite of rooms where the action was taking place and handed it to Harry. He paid his debt to society and we were off for Beaver Island with a couple of the same guys that would not allow him to leave the room.

In February 1955, our number 2 son Mark, not yet born, was in aviation terms, parked in "Donna's hangar," ready to be rolled out on the "ramp," when I got a call from Harry stating that the group wanted to go to the Island for that day and return the next.

This was good! I loaded them in the Bamboo Bomber and off we went. The weather reporting in that part of the world was almost nonexistent during those days, so the procedure was to go until you had to turn around, if necessary. With the typical dreary winter overcast covering the Island and fair visibility, we landed with no problem in about an inch of fresh snow. That night it snowed huge snowflakes like a bat out of Hell with the wind howling. The ceiling and visibility came down and stayed down the whole next day and next night. Being stranded on Beaver Island with my wife getting close to a delivery was not a position I cared to be in, but one that was my reality. The passengers were happy campers and thought all of this was just great. They couldn't have cared less if the snow lasted a month! Finally on the third day, the weather broke and a cold clear blue sky could be seen.

I was staying in Bub's cabin and though the snowplow had cleared the local roads, it became apparent that I would have to talk the plow operator into a trek to the airport to plow enough of a runway for a takeoff. He was glad to assist, so off we went in his huge truck, with me riding shotgun. On arrival, what I saw was not a good view. The Cessna UC78 was literally buried under a snowdrift-curved mound. I could see the top of the very small utility terminal building and that was all. The plow operator removed the snow from around the aircraft as best as he could, then he went on to preparing a single strip, not too much wider than the wings from where it was parked. I shoveled like hell to get the snow off the top of the flying machine. The direction of flight during the takeoff was already determined. Cross wind effect was of little concern, since the snow was considerably higher than the aircraft and with the tunnel effect, the cross wind was not an issue until liftoff. I could just about chin myself from the propellers due to the thick oil used in the radial engines. Of course the subfreezing temperature rendered the aircraft battery useless and would require a charging. Returning to town with the removed battery, the plow operator dropped me off at Bub's who of course was trying to stay warm in his cozy house since the cab business was not booming that time of year. He had a battery charger and I proceeded to charge up the battery. The next important step was to visit some neighbors and gather up as many blankets and extension cords as we could find, plus a couple electric bathroom heaters.

The Bamboo Bomber was parked about 100 feet from a small shed that had 110 volts power supply inside. My plan was to create a couple of tents around one of the engines using blankets, then place the electric heater under the tent to preheat the engine. At best I could do a job of heating up one and pray that the other one would eventually start, once I got a generator online. When the whole engineered heating system was complete and power was turned on, the high setting on the bathroom heater, was probably less than the lowest normal setting due to the voltage drop from the extension cord length. At any rate, though there was no possibility of getting the engines started that day, at least in my mind I felt I was doing something positive toward getting home to Donna.

The weather the next morning was just as bitter cold but flying out was a definite possibility. I had already given my passengers a heads-up to be ready if all worked out well. They indicated that they would be at the Shamrock, standing by for Bub to come back into town and pick them up, if my plan was successful. Harry made it very clear that if we had to stay a couple of extra days, that I should not concern myself, since they were all having a good time.

Bub drove me to the airport with the battery that I promptly reconnected. I discovered that I could actually pull through the starboard engine in a normal manner after the tented engine was heated. We then pulled the port engine through well over twenty five times in an attempt to limber it up, on the premise that if I could get the starboard engine started and a generator on line, I could eventually make the port engine fire up. When put to the task, the old Jacobs engines came to life. Starting the port engine was not an easy chore but ultimately was successful. With both engines warming up, I sent Bub back into town to drag the guys out of the barroom and board the airplane with me to get the Hell off the Island. Knowing full well who I was dealing with, I told Bub that I would keep the engines running for a maximum of exactly one hour, at which point I would leave without them. He told them – I waited an hour – then promptly departed through that huge tunnel of snow and off the island – with myself as the sole occupant of N51270 and back to the warm arms of my beautiful wife Donna. She delivered shortly thereafter.

THE BEAVER ISLAND TERMINAL BUILDING STILL EXISTS TO
THIS DAY
Charlene Wilson Collection

The trips with Harry were always interesting and I certainly appreciated his business in those lean years. The chances are good that everyone who has ever started their own business will never forget their early customers who helped shove food under the door. To my enjoyment, I have been able to savor interesting memories of those days. I'll wrap up these escapades by mentioning two additional events.

Though Harry's drinking episodes were legend, as previously noted, I never witnessed him stagger. There were some other effects however, that I did discover. One involved a payment check that Harry issued to me for charter service that was stamped rejected and returned to me from our First National Bank of Three Rivers. Information stated that it was not valid and would not be deposited to my account. I decided that if this was any indication of things to come, I had better delve into the situation. I immediately visited with

Al Renshaw who was the Bank Vice President, a great individual and someone whom I admired. He once told me to never lose my sense of humor that to this day, I feel was a great piece of advise. Mr. Renshaw offered the explanation that the reason for his bank not honoring this particular check from Harry was that it was "the wrong signature". When I queried further as to what constituted the "right signature," he stated in confidence that they had an arrangement with Harry that provided two examples of signatures. One was his "sober signature" and the other was his "drunken signature." Presumably this special service for one of their best clients was to prevent him from making a gigantic mistake on some stupid business transaction. Keep in mind that this occurred in the early 1950's when banking was done on a very personal level in small towns. Mr. Renshaw told me that he would advise the accounting department that any check written from Harry to me would never be questioned. It never was!

Then there was the trip to Beaver Island when Harry and his German Sheppard dog were the only passengers on board. Somewhere around Traverse City, Harry, sitting in the copilot seat, started talking about a subject that I did not like to hear. The gist of the message was that he and his friends were giving me a lot of charter business and further indicated that they had all "talked it over" and felt that they should get a price break. During that era, according to one of my old charter brochures that I have retained all of these years, this particular trip was about 250 miles one-way or 500 miles round-trip at 18 cents per air mile. The total was approximately $90.00. I queried, "Harry, what do you feel you should be paying me?" He responded. "We feel we should pay no more than $115.00." I commented. "Do you mean then, that if I agree to this price and bill you the $115.00 starting today, that this will be the end of that and I will never have to hear any more about this subject?" He nodded yes – we shook hands and I billed him the corrected amount from then on. Sometimes it's just better to give in!

How one learns to be a successful businessman with no formal education can be a most interesting process. A number of individuals stand out as having superb business mentoring skills that affected my life but one certain gentleman, now deceased, always comes to the front of my mind. His name is Ray Clifton. Mr. Clifton was a rather gruff diminutive person but very respected by his own employees. He was affectionately called "The Old Man." Mr. Clifton was owner of Clifton Engineering Company, a successful businessman, and a millionaire. He purchased a brand new Cessna 195 as his first company aircraft. Not being an aviator himself, he hired an excellent company pilot by the name of Ray June. I sold them aviation gas and did some of the maintenance on the 195. Additionally, they used my charter service from time to time. One cannot imagine how financially lean the months were operating during those winters at a small Michigan airport. One thing though I could always count on. When an invoice was mailed to Clifton Engineering, a payment in full was always received in the mail, just a couple of days later. As an expression of appreciation, I decided to call on Mr. Clifton at his office. Having never been there previously, I was escorted into his oak paneled office by his very efficient secretary. There the "Old Man" sat, behind the largest solid walnut desk I have ever seen in my life even to this day, perhaps his body size in comparison had something to do with my memory of the event. I explained to him that the reason I was there was to express my thanks for his business, and especially to let him know how much I appreciated the fact that he paid his bills on the day he received them. After my doing so, he proceeded to divulge the surprising fact that he had once declared bankruptcy while in his early years of business. He proudly pointed out to me the fact that he ultimately backtracked and paid off sums of dollars to the persons who lost money because of his going out of business. Mr. Clifton then proceeded to let me know that he made a pledge to himself that if he ever got out of the jam he was in at the time, that he would henceforth pay his bills on the day he received them. He then stood up on his feet behind his desk and while pointing his finger directly at me said these words. "Dick – I recommend that you do exactly that!" I left Mr. Clifton's office with a brand new business insight that helped me through my many years in business, and to this day, I still pay my bills on the day that they are received. In my consulting business, I continue to pass along the "Old Man's" philosophy to my clients. Imagine the impact of receiving one's financial statement with no accounts payables depicted. I've heard the argument that by using this technique, the "float" is lost. Think about it! Interest on the float is only a single event. Paying at the end of the invoice terms provides no repetitive advantage whatsoever. Admittedly, paying an invoice at the beginning of a cycle may lose you a token amount of interest but it is a one-time front-end expenditure. Never again will the interest gain be repeated. In the meantime you generate your business associates' respect along with its related buying power and public relations advantages. Then too, if one's business really hiccups, there is a 30-day built in grace period.

A persons credit standing holds hands with their honesty!

By: Author

The "Ten Percent For Love" rule – is another personal experience that I placed into my business philosophy envelope and still use to this day. It was gleaned in the early 1950's during a meeting at the Three Rivers Chamber of Commerce. As the Airport Manager I presented a short report on the progress of our local airport activities. The last speaker on the agenda was our fairly new City Manager, Cliff Miles. I personally had Cliff pegged as a dynamic manager and very much respected him for his no-nonsense, get things done skills.

To mentally set the scene, picture a substantial group of local merchants listening to his presentation about the operations and planning of city affairs, some of which might have an effect on their respective businesses. As Cliff spoke, I noted that something wasn't just right! A distracting buzz was occurring in the audience even as Cliff continued his presentation, caused from conversations between a number of the merchants. In those days, the storeowners on our small main street wielded a huge ration of influence around town. The moment Cliff's presentation was complete, one of those who had been whispering among themselves, stood on his feet and proceeded to verbally harpoon him on the subject of a his policy of not purchasing 100% of all of the City's goods and services from the local vendors, just as all of his predecessors apparently had done. On and on it went with many other merchants getting in their licks. To this point, the conversation was all one sided. Finally there was a lull in the conversation and with complete composure Cliff stated the following: "OK folks! While you were talking I got to thinking that you could have a point here. But first let me help you understand why I started making some of our purchases out of town. One of my jobs is to save our taxpayers' money and with some of the ridiculous charges you were making to the City, it became obvious we were able to save substantial amounts by going elsewhere. Nevertheless, I understand your feelings and I am prepared to provide a compromise. From this date forward, *I'll go ten percent for love, but damn it, don't you ever try me for eleven.*" With that said, Cliff stormed out of the room. To my knowledge, there was never another word uttered around town about this subject during his term as City Manager.

How very profound this rule really was. We all have been faced with similar situations when making purchases from persons and vendors whom we personally know. Initiating the Cliff Miles "Ten Percent For Love" rule in these circumstances makes good ethical sense.

The business of flight instructing touched my life in a very lasting way. Hardly any flight instructor ever forgets his or her early students. One such student of mine in the early 1950's was Lynn Herschleb. Lynn won an essay contest that I conducted for the students of the local high school. Winning this contest permitted him to solo at no charge and during that time, I hired him as a line boy. Lynn later went to Pittsburgh Institute Of Aeronautics and had an illustrious career with such things as flying a corporate jet for the Red Lobster Company chain. Another person who comes to mind is Bill Nagle, retired and living in this area. When in a group, Bill always introduces me as "his first flight instructor." We both know what special meaning this has. Then on occasion I hear a new voice from the distant past. Recently, I had a personal visit from my very first student pilot after starting the flight school at Three Rivers. Don Houseworth received his first flight lesson from me on May 20th, 1952. It is noted in my flight log. Don, now 67, went on to engage in an illustrious Air Force pilot career. He is an active sailplane pilot and I am now urging him to select a classic warbird aircraft of some sort, so he may continue to paint the sky.

Does each Airman let their mind take wing, as oft as I?
I think they do, but then...
So must the adventurers of the sea... the road...
perhaps all of mankind!
Frustrated earthlings – we airmen become artists while on high
Obsessed with God's canvas spread above and below... our
minds create poems.
We set words to symphonic sounds, silent to other ears on board
our fragile machine, while our mind's eye captures fleeing
ballads and scenes
I think to myself, I'll record on paper each of these trillion
thoughts, but this pledge never comes true, because earth
clutches my body far too soon
The answer for my frustration is always clear
I must always return to the air where I can delight in viewing the
sights and thoughts
provided by God

By: Author

The goings on in life through the years enriches my memories far beyond that which one person deserves. For example, I think of Colonel Roscoe Turner, Al Williams, Charles Lindberg, Wylie Post... these were the typical aviators I looked up to while growing up. Little did I know that in later years, I would be privileged to meet and know Roscoe Turner during the course of operating my own aircraft business in Three Rivers.

Born in 1895, Roscoe bought a WWI Jenny, adopted a uniform and formed the "Roscoe Turner Flying Circus." In 1928 he went to work for Howard Hughes on the movie set of Hell's Angels and pursued other movie flying parts in ensuing years. His illustrious air racing also started about this time and in 1932 through 1938 he won both the Thompson and Bendix races, flying his Wendell-Williams racer under the Gilmore Oil name. Who of my generation can ever forget seeing "Gilmore," his pet lion that flew with him on occasion, sporting his very own parachute? Colonel Turner established Roscoe Turner Aeronautical in 1941 and trained 3,300 pilots for the government. The postwar years brought his fixed base operation into a modern era when his company became the Beechcraft Distributor for the State of Indiana and later became one of my own company's Ward Aero, Inc. Warehouse Parts Distributors.

I first met Colonel Turner in the early 1950's while demonstrating to him a product I developed and patented. It was an emergency electrical and vacuum system for the single engine Beech Bonanza. I termed it "Turbo-Volt." This was an adaptation of my very first Ward Aero product a wind driven generator already being successfully marketed. Necessity being the mother of invention, the following episode pushed me into developing "Turbo-Volt."

At night during a light rain I took off on runway 23 from Three Rivers, Michigan in my Model 35 Beechcraft Bonanza N2830V. Fortunately I was alone. Just after entering the overcast at a few hundred feet, all of lights on the instrument panel and radio lights went to extreme bright. This was not a good sign! Grabbing my flashlight, I was able to shut down both the generator and the master switch and climb up to a safe altitude to provide some ground clearance, while trying to figure out what was happening. Being off-airways I had originally planned to get in the air to make radio contact with Goshen Radio along the way to pick up a clearance enroute to my destination. Lest you are looking down your young nose at me for using this procedure, note that this was a routine practice of that era. In fact it was perfectly legal to fly IFR enroute to a destination while remaining off-airways at an odd (easterly) or even (westerly) heading with no communications whatsoever. We're talking 4 course low frequency range days here!

Communications with any ground station at that moment was not high on my priority list. From what I could guess, (later proving to be correct), the generator field must have shorted to ground, thereby imposing an unregulated spike of voltage that fried the electrical system. Reluctantly, I turned on the battery switch only for a moment and took inventory of the situation. The voltage surge wiped out any lights that were on as well as the old Lear LTRA6 Omni scope. For reasons I still do not understand, the Lear transceiver still operated, probably because they used vacuum tubes instead of transistors, so I was able to use the low frequency receiver. The trick here was to do so without running down what was left of the battery which had already probably started to boil while the overvoltage activity took place. My best bet was to head for Battle Creek, located about 40 miles to the northeast. The south leg of the Battle Creek Low Frequency (LF) range would have to be captured using an aural signal of the beam, and that's what I did. By flipping the radio power on to listen, then off to save what little battery power that was left, I was able to bracket the beam and ride it in to the cone of silence. With no interest in jeopardizing any remaining power, I hand cranked the landing gear down. I was never able to communicate with Battle Creek, due to the high battery drain required to transmit. Things worked out during the approach where I spotted the ground lights at several hundred feet and was able to zigzag my way to the threshold of the runway after reaching the Low frequency station cone of silence. After landing, a phone call to the tower operator to explain the incident was received with understanding and sympathy. I imposed on an old friend, Whitey McLeod of Battle Creek Flying Service to transport me back to Three Rivers, via the concrete beam.

Daybreak comes quietly
Sneaking up on the dark
The sun finally commands the earth
I hope my controller had a good night

By: Author

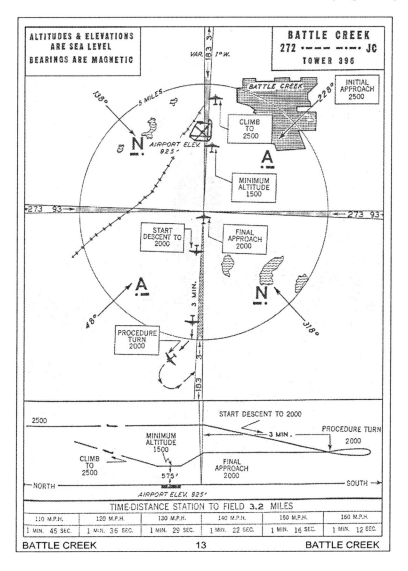

BATTLE CREEK MICHIGAN LOW FREQUENCY
FOUR COURSE RANGE – CIRCA 1955
R. Ward Collection

Never wanting to be placed in this position again, I designed, constructed, and installed the "Turbo-Volt" Emergency Electrical and Vacuum system on N2830V. The basic power was derived from one of my 12 Volt, 15Amp wind driven generators and the vacuum source from an 8-inch suction venturi tube. It worked like a champ. Pull a lever, out it came and you were back in business with oodles of electric power.

Patent # 3,069,116

TURBO-VOLT – EMERGENCY ELECTRICAL AND VACUUM SYSTEM
R. Ward Collection

It was during one of my "Turbo-Volt" sales visits to Roscoe Turner Aeronautical in the early part of the 1950's where I had my first opportunity to meet and visit with the famous Roscoe Turner. As old time aviators went, he was and still is high on my list. Flamboyant would be an understated word for this fine gentleman. His appearance to me was as I imagined and he made me feel at home for a generous amount of time in his office, adorned with artifacts from his earlier days.

From time to time, we would speak on the phone, or I would pay my respects during a short visit to his facility. Then in the mid-

50's my phone rang at the airport and Roscoe was on the other end. Something I never knew up to that point and later learned was that he was somewhat of a civic minded individual who had his own way of helping others out. These were his words: "Dick! I need your help!" I then discovered that he was quite involved in trying to assist convicts coming out of prison to make a new life for themselves in society. He stated that there was a young man, an ex-Marine, who was sent to a Federal Penitentiary in Chillicothe, Ohio for stealing while in the service. In due time, he was enrolled in an Aircraft and Engine Mechanic School as part of his rehabilitation process and would receive his FAA A&E mechanic license. Roscoe was tracking this individual's life, and in an attempt to help him go straight he contacted me. I was being asked to hire him, on the premise that he could be paroled, if he could become gainfully employed. Frankly, I did not need another employee at this stage of the development of Ward Aero, Inc. but if you think I was going to say no to Colonel Turner, you can think again. The answer was an emphatic yes. No doubt about it, this to my way of thinking would be my introduction into the world of humanitarianism accompanied by all of the fuzzy feelings thereby associated. Unfortunately, it did not work out just that way, but it sure provided me with one of life's experiences, and one that I will never forget.

A couple of days prior to the release of the ex-convict named Charles Poynter, I got a call from Roscoe telling me what time Poynter would arrive in Three Rivers at the Greyhound Bus Station. He would have the clothes on his back and a few bucks in his pocket. The rest was up to me. I had already decided in my own mind that I would only divulge his history to a single individual, in order to give him every opportunity to lead a normal life in our small community of about 7,000 people. That individual was our Chief of Police Jesse Younts. I saw no reason to even tell my wife. Pointer's parole officer did give me a call to make certain that I had his name and phone number on file. Interestingly when I relayed how all of this happened, his parting words were that "I had about a 30 percent chance of reforming this guy" and he wished me well. My experience was destined to be in the other 70 percent.

69

An old Dodge airport courtesy car was made available for Poynter to purchase through a payroll deduction. I then arranged to have him stay in a local rooming house. Poynter arrived on schedule, got settled and started to work in my maintenance shop. Though a good looking well-mannered individual, he had extremely poor work skills and always seemed to be on the defensive when attempts were made toward teaching him the precise world of aviation mechanical objectives and techniques. He was also quite "edgy" for lack of a better word.

I had a competitor, an FBO in Sturgis, Michigan, a small airport only about 15 miles from Three Rivers, by the name of Ed Shimp who owned Sturgis Aviation. Though we were friendly, Ed was never one of my favorite people, since he had a habit of stealing my mechanics, and did so with no apologies on three different occasions. He would offer them about 10 or 15 cents per hour more than I could pay in my early years of business, and I discovered early in the game that employee loyalty could rapidly disappear when money becomes involved. So it went with Chuck Poynter. No notice nor even a goodbye... just a call from his Parole Officer telling me that Poynter had changed jobs and it was OK with him, because he was still employed in the same county.

A month or so later, after arriving in the early morning at my small airport office terminal building, I discovered some broken glass and an open door. You guessed it. I had been robbed. Only petty cash was stolen from the till, and nothing else of value except it was noted that a substantial number of company payroll checks were missing. Being sequentially numbered, I immediately stopped payment that very moment by calling the First National Bank of Three Rivers, Michigan. The observant policeman inspecting the break-in made an interesting discovery. The broken glass opening in the door was not of sufficient size to get one's hand through to open the latch. He indicated that this might be a subterfuge and surmised that a key must have been used. Could it be? It could, and it was! I picked up the phone, called Ed Shimp and while starting to query him about Poynter; he asked me if I had seen him, since he had not reported to work for several days. It then came out that he also had also been robbed and someone had stolen some expensive radios, among other things. I could not resist passing on a comment something along the lines of "Ed! This is payback time for you stealing my help." Then I told him the whole story. Shimp never hired anyone else from me after that, and we remained friendly through the following years until his passing on.

It was pretty easy to track the route traveled by Chuck Poynter. With the stolen Ward Aero, Inc. payroll checks, he would write himself a check, sign my name on the bottom and after showing him his identification, would find some poor guy to cash it. I was receiving calls along the route of his travel from people who wanted to know why my company checks were not clearing. Though I felt bad for their losses, there was nothing either my bank or I could do to help those getting fleeced. The route took him north through Lower Michigan to the Upper Peninsula, then south through Chicago, ultimately to Louisville, Kentucky. That is where he reportedly was apprehended riding out of a motorcycle shop that he had just broken into on a brand new stolen motorcycle. It was back to jail for Poynter. Laid end to end by date sequence, one could see that he gave himself a raise on every payroll check that he wrote. Since he was convicted on a felony in that jurisdiction, plus his history of parole violation, there would be no need for me to further press charges. Or so I thought!

That could be the end of this story but hold on to your hat. About 9 or 10 months later, I was visiting and enjoying an early evening dinner with my friend and business associate T.W. Smith and his wife at the old terminal building at Cincinnati, Ohio's Lunkin Airport. Smitty, now retired, used to own T. W. Smith Aircraft, a large engine overhaul shop in Cincinnati. Sitting to my left were a bunch of the local airport crowd whom it seemed to me were typical and I say this with respect and affection – "airport bums." Out of the corner of my ear I heard a familiar name brought up from the midst of the group at the other table. The name? Chuck Poynter! Smitty knew most of the guys sitting there and at my request he introduced me to them. With very little small talk, I queried them about this fellow with the name Poynter. They said that he was a new mechanic on the field who had just started doing maintenance out of the trunk of his car. Apparently his shop rates were pretty good, considering the overhead. His description fit to a tee. Excusing myself, I ran to the pay phone in total disbelief to make a phone call to our Police Chief Jesse Younts, and report that Poynter had broken out of jail. Jesse told me to stand by the phone to further assist him, while he contacted the Cincinnati authorities. A short time later, he called back with some earthshaking news. Charles Poynter had already served some jail time and was once again out on parole.

If that doesn't ruin a person's day, get this. About a year later, I got a phone call from none other than Poynter. He was in some place or the other and was setting up a new aircraft shop. One of my Ward Aero, Inc. product lines was line of aircraft jacks. This jerk actually had the gall to ask me if I would sell him a set of my jacks at a discount. My memory is not precise after these many years but I think my response went along the lines of, "Poynter – if you ever show your face in my town again, be prepared to die!"

The ultimate result from this experience does not diminish in any way, my great respect for Colonel Roscoe Turner. He gave it his best shot, as did I. It just did not work out in this instance, but the episode sure adds some texture to the woof and weave of the fabric of my life.

There are no clouds in the sky
The wind is but a whisper over my wings
Lakes glitter and birds circle below
It's a good day to electrocute Charles Manson

By: Author

COLONEL ROSCOE TURNER – CIRCA 1939
Roscoe Turner Quote
"There is no excuse for an airplane, unless it goes fast."
Daryl Groves Collection

COLONEL ROSCOE TURNER'S WINGS UNIFORM PATCH
R. Ward Collection

CHAPTER VI
LIFE BEYOND FLYING

ENTER MANUFACTURING! During the early 1950's, the Ward Aero fixed base operation at the Three Rivers Airport enabled us to eke out a modest living that bordered on poverty. More than once, Donna pumped gasoline into an airplane while holding our firstborn son Dane in her arms while I was on a charter trip. We had each other and were in the process of raising a family. Donna never complained about my lack of participation in some family affairs, and I certainly never complained about her not complaining! Her domestic skills were exceeded only by her good looks.

Having moved my modest shop facility from its T-hangar location on the airport to a 40' x 80' building, I decided to apply to the Civil Aviation Administration (CAA), now the Federal Aviation Administration (FAA) to become a Certified Repair Station when none existed in our part of Michigan. There was little reason to do this other than the challenge of doing so coupled with a little prestige. In my modest but growing shop, I was able to convince the CAA that I should have an unlimited Class I & III Airframe, an Unlimited Accessory, plus a Nondestructive Inspection Certificate. Try that today and see how far you get! It could never happen. My repair shop was modest but it was always hospital clean and well organized. My pride in workmanship apparently impressed our CAA inspectors, which may have been the reason why I was able to convince them to give me these unlimited ratings. As fate would have it, these ratings provided me with the opportunity to move on to bigger and better things, ultimately leading to my learning much about the manufacturing and remanufacturing of aircraft parts. This action moved forward the eventual growth of Ward Aero, Inc.

During that era, Continental Motors Corporation was located in Muskegon, Michigan. They, along with Lycoming Engine Company and to a lesser degree Franklin Air-Cooled Motors, provided all of the air-cooled aircraft engines used to power the majority of the general aviation fleet. One day out of the clear, I received a call from Bill Deam, who ran the Duke Harrah Company in Niles, Michigan. They were heavy into the military aviation surplus business and were suppliers of original equipment to Continental. Bill said that Mr. Ramsey, the director of purchasing of Continental Motors heard about me and wanted to know if I would be interested in discussing the possibility of Ward Aero remanufacturing their aircraft electrical accessories that included starters, generators and magnetos. Bill was a Hell of a salesman who taught me a lot about buying and selling in the aircraft surplus marketplace during our association. Such things as: "Never speak out of the side of your mouth, unless you're from Texas." "When you speak on the phone to someone on the east coast, make it fast, but when you speak to someone in the south or southwest, always ask how their family is doing," or, "Buy yourself an old funeral hearse – it makes a great truck for hauling airplane parts." Some of his teachings rubbed off, but I drew the line on purchasing a hearse.

Within a couple of days, I decked myself out in the only suit that I owned, and traveled with Bill Deam to meet Mr. Ramsey. Bill suggested that Ramsey had an ongoing affair with "Jim Beam", and suggested it might be a good investment for me to consider, so we purchased a fifth of booze on the way to Muskegon. We walked through the reception area directly into Ramsey's huge office and I was introduced. Shaking hands with my right hand, I sat the booze on Ramsey's desk with my left, feeling like a damn fool. Ramsey smiled at Bill! I deplored what I had just done and made a spot decision never to play that game again, and to this day, I never have.

What I discovered at this meeting was that skilled workers who had been performing this same operation for many years were overhauling all of their aircraft accessories in-house at the Getty Street engine test house in Muskegon, Michigan. In their questionable wisdom United Auto Workers (UAW) union leaders pronounced that Continental's management would have to cave in to their unrealistic demands by selecting the overhaul technicians from their own union list, based purely on seniority rather than personal workman skills. This work, being a skilled job certainly demanded some specific skills. Continental management would have none of a plan to move a floor sweeper into a skilled position, just because he excelled in the number of years he was with the company. A decision had already been made by Continental to subcontract the whole project out. Enter Ward Aero!

What I knew about aircraft accessories being produced in this volume could be placed on the head of a pin, but I sure didn't let Ramsey know that. Then there was the matter of how much I would charge. This, as luck would have it, turned out to be the least of my worries. Ramsey simply told me how much they would pay, and that was that. The figures still linger in the corner of my mind. A flat parts and labor rate of $16.72 for a Generator and $14.50 for a starter would be paid. What made this possible was that we were permitted to co-mingle parts and at our option could declare the unairworthy residue to be "beyond economical repair." This eliminated the necessity of requiring the purchase of major components, such as an armature. Another big plus was that we were immediately provided with tremendous purchasing power by being able to purchase on an original equipment manufacturing (OEM) basis directly from Delco-Remy Division of General Motors and Bendix Corporation. This buying power proved to be a real windfall, when our own Ward Aero line of exchange accessories was later introduced to the marketplace through a warehouse distribution system. That visit with Ramsey was a great day, but the real world of the manufacturing business was about to be introduced to me.

With little more that hand tools in the shop, it became necessary to immediately outfit it with such things as a spray booth, which we constructed ourselves, as well as electrical test machines that I was able to lease. Two weeks to the day, after the meeting with Ramsey, a semi-truck arrived with skids of hundreds of accessories, which for the most part were partially disassembled. We call them "basket cases" in the trade. With only a couple of employees, sleeping hours at night were in short supply. How I ever worked through all of this is a mystery to this day. I'll always believe, as I previously alluded to, that luck was the largest factor. The harder I worked, the luckier I got!

This association with Continental Motors continued for many years and true friendships were made with the grassroots guys at the Getty Street Test House. Key people such as Art Vandenberg, and Lloyd Raymond, will forever be remembered for their understanding and assistance. In essence, they protected me from our competitors taking over this business. Ward Aero, Inc. did an excellent job at a reasonable price, and our quality was outstanding. Art and Lloyd who were real aircraft engine men knew this and appreciated the fact. Others around the factory were always hanging around looking for a personal payoff, a game I absolutely refused to play. As an example, one day between Christmas and New Years I was visiting the Test House. Other vendors would pay a courtesy call on Mr. Ramsey, the Purchasing Director, but I could not stand the corrupt guy, so through the years, I avoided him like the plague. On this particular day, I received word from several persons at the Test House that Mr. Ramsey wanted to see me at his office in the main plant, as soon as I showed up at the Test House. Having little choice I entered Ramsey's office and approached his desk. I noticed how clean the surface was, save a single Christmas card laying in the middle. It was one of my personal Christmas cards that had been sent to a number of persons at Continental. Ramsey did not offer to shake my hand, but merely stated the following, while pointing to the card; "Ward, I got this from you in the mail, but I want you to know that "you can't drink Christmas cards!" I replied; "Ramsey, that may be true, but you sure as Hell can eat one…I suggest you try it!" and strode out of his office. I never was called back to his office. For some reason, even though he had the power to do so, he never replaced us as a vendor.

During those early business years, with the framework of production techniques established plus our OEM buying power, it struck me that mechanics might accept the premise of an exchange program on such things as starters, generators and magnetos. With a faulty unit in hand, they could order a remanufactured unit, then send in their defective unit (Core) later. At that point in time, there was no such concept in the aircraft industry. With a modest start, working through Don Horn of the Don Horn Company, Dick Adams of Aviation Supply Company and Paul Bingaman of GASCO, the forerunner of Van Dusen Aircraft Supply, these warehouse distributors issued some purchase orders and took on a stock of units. Bingo! The exchange program took off like wildfire. Other distributors were added as were many other products, such as ignition harnesses, ground support equipment, Blo-proof exhaust gaskets, wheel and brake parts, etc. Ward Aero, Inc. grew and became very well known in the industry with marketing techniques being modeled to this day by others.

Some of my business philosophies were adapted from my observations of others. One such business technique that had to do with costing and establishing selling prices was gleaned from Thomas Edison. I call it the "Hog" theory of costing. I ask you: Have you ever seen a hog die a natural death?

The difficult question, when one is in business to make a profit is: "How should we price and/or discount our products and services?" We are able to arrive at satisfactory conclusions, but only after applying a huge ration of logic coupled with the usual accounting techniques. Costing is not the exact science many accountants would have us believe. When all of the textbook formulas have been applied, one final and most important test must be applied. Will the prices and discounts hold up under competition? That question must become part of any pricing formula. Those who do not go through this exercise are asking for trouble. Here is how I discovered Edison's wonderful logic.

In the mid 1950's I visited the Ford Museum in Dearborn, Michigan. Henry Ford and Thomas Edison were close friends. An admirer of Edison, I was drawn to the museum's collection of Edison's original writings. One letter in particular, dated 1891, demonstrated the inventor's profound wisdom. I was so impressed, I wrote it down word for word. Its wisdom became a business guideline I have followed even to this day. Edison wrote:

"Friend Marks,

To my mind the raising of the price of electricity from three-quarters to one cent per lamp hour is a bid for competition, <u>I am a believer in ensuring the permanency of an investment</u> by keeping prices so low that there is no inducement to others to come in and ruin it.

There seems to be a law in commercial things as in nature. If one attempts to obtain more profit than general average, he is immediately punished by competition."

In other words, Edison was telling Marks (an apparent employee or business associate), "Look here my friend, we're making a good living selling electricity for three-quarters of a cent per lamp hour, why should we play hog and get eaten by our competition?" Smart man, that Thomas Edison. I have condensed these words down farther to: <u>*My daddy told me he ain't never seen a hog die a natural death*</u>.

Has anything changed since 1891? Absolutely not! Edison may not have had direct competition at the time he wrote those words, but you can bet your life that there would have been someone lying in the weeds ready to take him on.

DEVELOPMENT AND ENGINEERING COSTS

When the price of a new product is conceived, development and engineering costs must be amortized over some chosen number of units. Does this ever drop off the line as a lower unit price to the consumer? Rarely! Just how long can one get away with applying these associated costs to a given product? If given their druthers, the bean counters in the accounting department would love to see this burden live on forever. But once these charges are paid off, there is a golden opportunity to reduce sales prices or offer longer discounts in order to prevent having *"others come in and ruin it."*

ADMINISTRATIVE OVERHEAD

Standard costing techniques dictate that administrative charges are applied to every project. It takes a certain amount of money from the kitty each day to pay the rent, heat, light, telephone, insurance, administrative and sales costs. This shows up as a percentage factor that is normally applied in the costing process. Does this mean that this percentage always has to be charged to every new costing project? No way! There is no logical reason one could think of for not bringing certain projects in line with lower-than-usual prices in order to compete, once you have covered the costs of placing the key in the company door each day (operating overhead). It's better to have a bunch of little deals going quite well, than always having to struggle in an effort to make the big deal work. Low prices consistent with quality *"ensures the permanency of an investment."*

Businesses come and go for a variety of reasons. Without quality and service, they rapidly become dead in the water. Pricing the product to attain a reasonable profit is the next critical element. When quality and service are equal among competitors, then price becomes king.

What is a reasonable profit? If 10 business people were asked to give their definition of a reasonable profit, you would get 10 different answers. It's really how much they agree with Tom Edison.

Those who live in the past never change their price structure to keep up with Edison's *"law in commercial things."* Continually analyzing the competition's prices and discounts is as important in running a business as borrowing money. People operating companies while not involving themselves personally in viewing competition on a perpetual basis, should do so immediately to see what is really going on.

During my many years in business, I have seen a tremendous change in the distribution of goods and services. In today's highly competitive business world, one must be instantly responsive to market force variations as they occur.

I suggest if you are directly involved in sales, service or manufacturing pricing, you should look beyond textbook accounting theories and consider Tom Edison's guidelines when establishing prices. This could go a long way toward *"ensuring the permanency of your investment."*

Pricing is one important facet of running a business but sound marketing techniques are equally important. Persons far smarter than this writer have written volumes on the subject, but certain basics should always prevail. Many businesspersons will attempt to shove concepts down the consumer's throat in the interest of profit, instead of tailoring the marketing to make the consumer feel that they have experienced an enjoyable buying experience.

Here is but one example of an "in your face" marketing ploy that I believe will backfire. It refers to a letter to the Editor quoted below that I recently mailed to a few newspapers in our locale. Following the publications a number of persons called and congratulated me for taking the time to express the feelings they themselves had. They felt exactly as I but did not take the time to complain. As to whether or not my small contribution will change the tide remains to be seen but I guarantee that the movie managers heard from a number of others who read my words. I mailed clippings to the president of Goodrich Quality Movie, Inc., of course, along with a few choice hand-written words. The article read:

PAID MOVIE ADVERTISING – ENOUGH ALREADY!

For more years than you wish to hear about, almost every Friday, my wife and I have a "date night." Routinely, we go to a late afternoon movie and then have dinner at a restaurant of our choice. Last Friday we went to the Three Rivers 6 owned by the Goodrich Quality Movie, Inc. chain. The movie, advertised to start at 6:05 imposed on our patience with a seemingly never-ending series of paid advertisements. I'm not talking about previews of coming attractions or an ad to push their popcorn here. I mean a ration of genuine hard-core repetitious commercial name brand ads. Finally after about 20 minutes of this garbage, around 6:25 we got to see the show that we paid to see.

After stewing about the fact that I actually paid money to have this junk thrown at me, I decided to vent my spleen to the Manager. I did so by telling him that I have no desire to spend my money to patronize any movie that subscribes to these tactics. Further, asking for him to pass along my objection to the corporation hierarchy got me a jaundiced look and the following comment: "Sir, There's nothing that I can do about this. It's all about money!" I responded with, "Indeed it is, and that includes the lack of mine that you will be receiving, unless this nonsense is scuttled." I also passed along to him the fact that an employee I spoke to working for a competitive Kalamazoo movie confided in me some time ago by saying that each time they try to shove this concept down the public's throat the public reaction was less than positive and they backed down.

If these Goodrich Company fools want to continue with their folly, then a fair compromise would be for them to advertise two starting times. One for the paid ads and the other for when the previews and movie starts. When I suggested this solution to the manager, it was obvious to me that he was not writing down any notes. To conclude the conversation, I did mention that I would concede another 60 seconds watching the popcorn ad and then waved Adios!

As this is being written, Donna and I are enjoying a month in Palm Springs, California. Published in today's "Desert Sun" newspaper is a short and sweet display advertisement by the Century Theaters chain. It states: "*If you want to see commercials...watch TV. Never any TV commercials!*" Wonders will never cease. This company gets the picture and I have been vindicated.

I conclude with the following thought: "Mason said to Dixon, we've got to draw this darned line somewhere." I just did! Now how about some help from other moviegoers who despise this stealing of their time. When this stuff is forced upon each of us, speak up to the time thieves, and then patronize the movies that play fair with our money. They might just get the message.

Can we seemingly insignificant individuals make a difference, when things seem "not just right?" Indeed we can, as long as we don't try to push on a long rope expecting to see the other end of the rope move. It is far too easy for us to fall prey to what I call my "pushing on a rope" trap.

"When one pushes on a rope expecting to see the other end of the rope move, it almost never happens. To make the other end

of your rope move, cut it up into small pieces then push on each of the shorter pieces! You will see the other ends move a distance equal to the distance that you push each small piece. Amazingly, you will succeed in having pushed on the end of the long rope length but by doing so in small increments."

By: Author

There have been other incidents that have occurred that provided me with wisdom that would be used for the rest of my life. The following occurred during the year 1974, while attending one of the semiannual meetings of a high-powered trade organization I belonged to, namely the Aviation Distributors & Manufacturers Association (ADMA). The place was at the beautiful Broadmoor Hotel in Colorado Springs. The framework of ADMA then, and to this day, is constructed on the premise that key individuals from both the manufacturing as well as the distribution sectors of each member company join together in prearranged meetings to communicate and develop their products and marketing. The thing that makes it special is that only the top echelon personnel of each of the member companies are permitted in the organization. This results in high-level decisions being accomplished without committee action. This provided me with the following thought that I use to this very day: *"The best committee is a committee of one."*

Another feature of the meetings always involved a dynamic speaker who passed along words of wisdom that could be used in our businesses. That particular session included a motivational speaker who provided a number of his personal philosophies in promoting sales. He covered a lot of ground including his premise that any good salesman will *NEVER wear shoes that contain shoelaces.* As the talk progressed, he kept intertwining this statement with his other messages. Along the way virtually everyone was looking around to those seated near them to see who was and who was not wearing shoelaces. Thank God – I was wearing loafers.

Seated to my right was Pat Murphy, the Marketing Manager of Cooper Airmotive, Inc. Pat wore loafers. To my left sat the President of Van Dusen Aircraft Supply Corporation. You guessed it – he was wearing shoelaces. During the presentation, a scheduled coffee break took place. When we returned to our seats, we discovered that he had gone to his room and changed his shoes. This particular individual always played the part of presenting himself as the high-powered businessman who for me at least always seemed to believe himself to be a notch above his associates. This never did impress me, as this type of individual was never easy for me to get to know, let alone with whom I enjoyed doing business. At any rate, I spotted his shoe episode and decided to harpoon his self-righteous attitude by letting everyone sitting around us know that he went up to his room and changed his shoes. Instead of taking it on the chin and enjoying the moment as any regular guy would, he displayed his displeasure and disgust with us by sitting elsewhere, thereby providing me with a great amount of personal pleasure. At future meetings through the years, when I witness him acting like the big executive while basking in a feeling of his own power, I would always make it a point to tell this story to any group within ear shouting distance. I got the feeling that he did not like me very much!

As for me – to this very day, I refuse to own a pair of shoes that utilize shoelaces, and invariably look at a man's feet to see if he is a "good" salesman. Oh yes! In addition to checking for shoelaces, never hire a person for any responsible position who has a visible ornament protruding through their tongue, lip, or eyebrow. Equally important - if they are male, look to be certain they are wearing a shirt that contains a pocket with a pen or pencil protruding from within. If a female, come right out and ask – "Do you have a writing instrument and a piece of paper in that purse? If any of the forgoing concerns are not positive, you are asking for trouble. That individual has a severe complex and even worse, trusts their memory far too much.

The lessons learned have served me well. I'm still a pretty good salesman with no body pierced parts and would never be seen in public without a shirt pocket containing a writing instrument. Even more important, I continue to maintain my sense of humor.

> *While my thoughts should be on today*
> *My mind seems to journey toward yesterday*
> *If I should stall or lose my way*
> *I'll deny it*

By: Author

When business opportunities come along they simply must be considered. Chance comes into play here, but one must be able to recognize opportunities and capitalize on them as they occur. I have noticed that some people would not recognize a good deal if it swatted them over the head. I have also noticed that all too often persons will massage the transaction over and over in a seemingly endless exercise in procrastination, all the while asking their friends and relatives what they think of the idea. I believe the best way to move ahead in the business world is to single handedly make your decision. Of course there may be need for seeking advise from a lawyer, accountant, or a business consultant but that's about it. As a courtesy it might be nice to mention it in passing to one's spouse, but don't say, "What do you think?" My reasoning for this is simple. Our circle of loved ones, friends, and relatives feel honored to willingly provide their ration of opinions. The problem is that it is almost always tainted by the fact that they honestly do not want to see us fail. Offering positive encouragement places them at risk. Consider my advice. This technique has always served me well.

One such opportunity occurred in 1965 when I received a phone call and eventual visit from Al Korth. Al was a local self-made businessman who accumulated his fortune by first selling industrial steel off of the back end of his truck literally by himself. His company, Standard Steel Industries, eventually evolved into the business of design and construction of stadium bleachers. A few of his engineered designs and installations include the bleachers at Arizona State University in Tempe, as well as the Michigan International Speedway, and Western Michigan University.

Although at that time we had been in Three Rivers thirteen years and knew him by reputation, I simply had never met Al. To say that we traveled in different circles is a gross understatement. Al played golf - I did not. Al took Saturdays and Sundays off - I did not. Get the idea? What I did not know about Al was is that he used to be a Ryan ST primary flight instructor in WWII and had never flown after the war. Somehow he decided that it was high time for him to get back into the air. Fortunately, when he received his military discharge, he converted his military certificate into a civilian license including his instrument rating. Bringing him into modern aviation became a matter of modern equipment knowledge and some flying hours of practice for him. Although I still maintained my FAA Flight Instructor Certificate I had steered Ward Aero, Inc. toward the manufacturing aspects of my company. With my flight instructor rating, I was later able to legally check him out in our Cessna 310 Twin. He did quite well.

In our initial meeting, Al suggested that I consider joining in with him via a joint merger. I could sense that he was enticed by the fact that we operated a company twin-engine aircraft for our own use. Al's company, a closely held Corporation had huge assets compared to ours, but he was willing to provide me with shares of Standard Steel Industries, Inc. of a proportional amount. Another thing that I discovered in short order was that he was impressed with my organizational abilities by noting that I had developed a manual of procedure that would enable my company to literally continue operating in an efficient manner, in the event of my departure from the earth. Al personally did not have that capability and it became obvious that this would be one of my undertakings, in the event that we made the deal.

The deal we did. It occurred in the form of a stock swap with Standard Steel owning Ward Aero, Inc. and me owning shares of Standard Steel Industries, Inc. I became Vice President of Standard Steel while remaining President of Ward Aero, Inc. Al suggested that we construct a facility adjacent to the Standard Steel operation and move Ward Aero off of the airport. That suited me to a tee, inasmuch as we had completely outgrown the building at the airport and were faced with additional facilities in the near future anyhow.

**As a businessperson, never fall in love with the merchandise.
That even includes your own company**

By: Author

Although Ward Aero, Inc. was able to grow at a modest rate prior to the merger, making this move stepped things up and gave us the financial flexibility to develop more products at a rapid pace. For the first time in my life, I was able to utilize the full services from an inside CPA Controller who not only knew how to pinch pennies, but was able to get a real grasp on the nuances of the aviation industry. Tad Lenczycki a Polish immigrant survived Hitler's takeover and concentration camps. He taught me a lot about accounting that has served me well to this day. Keep in mind that when I first started in business, I used my "two spindle accounting technique." A bill comes in and it goes on one spindle. When it was paid, it goes on the other spindle. Any money left over could be used for expanding one's business or on rare occasion, to pay oneself. This system still works well for small operations and is highly recommended.

The innovative accounting technique that I engineered dealt with "core charges" that were affixed to the sale of our exchange aircraft accessories, such as magnetos, starters, generators, etc. Consider the premise of selling a remanufactured unit of any sort. The success of the continuation of the exchange program relies upon receiving a used unit back, so that the process can be repeated. During those days, exchanges were almost unheard of in the aircraft industry, since virtually everyone overhauled their own accessories in the field, or would replace them with new units. Today, it is commonplace. One of my personal satisfactions and claims to fame is that I designed and first started this process of marketing within the aviation industry.

The "hook" on this event from a bookkeeping viewpoint is the way that I handled the accounting prior to the merger. In simple terms, I considered the income from the sale of the exchange as pure income. The money received from the core charge went into a "core reserve" fund. This sum of money went on the books, but I did not pay any income tax on any of these dollars. I did so with the logic that it was money that I owed to my distributors. The dollars in this fund was always subject to recall at any time they stopped purchasing my exchanges. This creative approach generated a tremendous amount of cash reserve that kept growing and growing as I continued to appoint and stock my distribution network. There is little doubt that when this was explained to Al Korth he understood this event and his offer to trade stock also brought in a pile of cash. Keep in mind that the Ward Aero acquisition involved the book value of each company. Sitting in the bank was our growing pile of untaxed cash that could be used as one chose. Tad, his Controller also appreciated the framework of this creative accounting but confided in me that it might not hold up in an IRS audit. I stuck to my guns and continued the process. Wonder of wonders, a couple of years later we did have an IRS audit on just the Ward Aero, Inc. part of the company and it fell upon me to demonstrate how all of this works. Without going into great detail, I will tell you that it was one of the highlights of my life. The IRS agent came into our place of business at an appointed time and announced that he would be there for several days. He queried as to whether we could provide him with some office space from which he could carry on his work. I respectfully advised him that we would oblige and told our receptionist to place a small folding card table and a wooden chair up in the reception area directly in front of her position where the public came and went. Visitors of course had to walk around his "desk," but I considered that to be a minor inconvenience for the agent. He did not seem to be too happy, but I explained that we were short on space in the office but optionally could provide an actual desk in a part of our production area. After showing it to him, he elected to stay in the original spot. I don't think he liked the noise created by one of our generator test stands but that's only a guess. Though I showed him all of our file cabinets where records were kept and how our filing system worked, I got the impression that in his mind we were supposed to supply him with special secretarial services during his stay. I explained that our books are wide open to him and we have nothing to hide but we all had a business to run. I further told him that he had full access to our files and Xerox machine to run his own copies, while noting that if he had any pages come up blank, he should place them in a special folder since Xerox gave us a per page credit for any copies that did not properly feed through the machine. It took him the better part of a half-day to get settled in but I got the feeling that he was accustomed to a lot of this stuff being done for him. My attitude was – what the hell…we can all learn, and his time had come.

His second day started a little late. I don't know if he neglected to set his alarm or what, but when he finally did come in at midmorning he started searching through this and that. I got the feeling that it was a fishing expedition. Having been previously introduced to our Controller Tad, I overheard him query Tad if he planned on going to lunch. When Tad advised that his wife packed him a brown bag lunch the agent departed for an hour, but not before advising that he wanted us to demonstrate the "core charge" accounting process. This of course was the real reason the guy showed up to begin with. I had previously advised Tad to advise him that I was the only one qualified to explain this complicated process and to be sure to contact me after lunch. The scene was set.

I had already set the stage for a professional dog and pony show by spreading parts of all kinds of aircraft accessories around on my office floor that ranged from used parts and overhauled parts plus complete overhauled as well as brand new units that we had to secure to take care of those cores that were never returned or damaged beyond economical repair. I like flow charts so I drew up a generous supply of those as well. When he returned from lunch, my secretary showed him into my office and over about a two-hour period, in minute detail explained the complexities of an aircraft accessory exchange program, as designed by Ward. He would speak once in a while but I did most of the talking and of course reinforced his thoughts with such phrases as, "I'm certain that you understand how this part (or unit) moves along through the distribution system." It seemed odd to me that he did not ask many questions.

The next day, when he did not come to work, we removed his office furniture and never heard another word from he nor the IRS. Tad just shook his head! I think Al Korth was proud of me.

Those were the years of merger mania and at one point Al Korth called me into his office and explained that he had just received a communication and offer to merge with Medalist Industries, Inc. and that we should consider it. Listed on the American Stock Exchange,

Medalist Corporate headquarters in Milwaukee, Wisconsin was quite involved in the athletic equipment areas of manufacturing and made such things as baseball uniforms and even owned their own knitting mill. To my way of thinking, after all of the lean years, it was a great opportunity to become liquid but somewhat doubted that Medalist would want Ward Aero because of the lack of synergism. I correctly presumed what they really wanted was to enter into the stadium bleacher business and mentioned to Al that I would be willing to buy back Ward Aero rather than stand in his way, but would be delighted to have the opportunity to turn my assets into saleable stock if the deal went in that direction.

A meeting was arranged for a couple of weeks later and we ultimately met in Al's large office at Standard Steel with Mr. Fisher, the President of Medalist as well as his controller and the Medalist lawyer. Al had arranged to have his corporate lawyer there who drove down from Grand Rapids, Michigan plus of course Tad, our controller, and myself. Mr. Fisher had been able to make Medalist grow through some fifteen acquisitions and had already done his homework with all of the records and numbers we previously supplied. So much so, in fact, that in short order he had his lawyer present the framework of a buy/sell agreement to us for signatures right on the spot. "Take your time looking it over," Mr. Fisher said while relaxing on the sofa.

It did not take a wiz kid to see that his offer was fair and certainly would enhance our positions, but I decided to be very frank with Mr. Fisher about how Ward Aero, Inc. might fit into the picture. His comments were interesting. He stated to me that he had noted that we operated a company aircraft and that this was an area that he would find to be an asset. He commented further that he would want for me to take this obligation on as an extra duty and in fact preferred that we sell the Ward Aero/Standard Steel 310 Cessna and upgrade to a propjet. Hot dog!

Expecting to shake hands on the pending deal and let the hands of time take over, Mr. Fisher announced that our two lawyers should get together and spend as much time as necessary to fully develop the agreement and bring it back for signatures. Fisher's attorney nodded in agreement and our attorney mumbled some words to the effect that that was not possible since he had all of his information in his office in Grand Rapids and needed some time to complete the chore. What happened next was a textbook business lesson that I will never forget and worthy of being passed along.

With no hesitation, Mr. Fisher acknowledged that it might be more convenient if our attorney could work in his own office and asked me if I would consider flying the two lawyers to Grand Rapids. I said "of course." He further elaborated by telling them both that he understood that this would entail some overtime but to lock themselves in a room and call for me to pick them back up in the aircraft when the job was complete. Before our lawyer could comment through his clenched teeth, Mr. Fisher advised that he was very willing to pay them any hourly rate of money that they felt was fair and would honor the hourly price. While the two of them were talking in the hallway, Mr. Fisher commented on the fact that he performs this same action during each of his acquisitions. He said to us, "This might seem excessive to offer to pay them any per hour amount of money for which they ask, but look at it this way. We can roughly count the hours by how long they are gone. If we give them days or more probably weeks to go back and forth with their paper shuffle, they can and probably would skin us alive." He also elaborated on the fact that he has personally witnessed otherwise good transactions break down and go south while the attorneys start placing their individual clients into adversarial roles. Mr. Fisher further noted "There is also the reality that we are watching the clock and therefore the hourly rate becomes a mundane issue." Al and I both smiled and nodded our heads in agreement, as I moved them along to toward our local airport. Some six hours later, our attorney called me for their pickup in Grand Rapids and that evening back in Three Rivers we signed the buy/sell agreement.

Becoming a part of a large corporation enabled me to personally glean new knowledge. I learned what "home office charges" were for the first time in my life and soon discovered that the stock value is really what counts in bean counter circles. This was not all bad, since we merged at about eight bucks per share and I was able to sell a substantial block after a couple of years at over twenty four. I recommended that we purchase a Merlin II propjet for corporate transportation and talked the home office into picking up all of the fixed costs. Then, in order to increase the seat usage, I arranged it so any approved subsidiary president or manager who was approved so could schedule the use of the aircraft. The real innovation occurred when I circulated the schedule to the subsidiaries on a daily basis. This permitted anyone to bootstrap onto someone else's trip if it was going somewhere near the desired direction. The exception to this rule was when someone deemed the trip a VIP flight and in those cases, bootstrapping was not allowed. Our seat utilization drove upward and efficiency increased far beyond what I had expected. I'm proud to say that this was recognized in the aviation industry and ultimately recognized by the Ziff Davis publication "Business and Commercial Aviation" magazine, where I was presented with an award at the famous Reading Air Tradeshow. The plaque reads; "1972 BUSINESS FLYING AWARD Presented to *RICHARD I. WARD President of WARD AERO by FLYING and BUSINESS & COMMERCIAL AVIATION Publications of the Ziff-Davis Aviation Division".*

By 1967 it became obvious to me that our aircraft parts manufacturing division was an awkward fit within the framework of the Medalist group of companies and would eventually be spun off. The flight operation was virtually running like a well-oiled machine and needed little of my personal assistance, since I had already placed a full time company pilot on the payroll. In a confidential meeting with Mr. Fisher, I confirmed that this fact was inevitable and suggested to him that rather than offer Ward Aero for a sale through a business broker that I might be interested in purchasing the company back again. He suggested that if I had interest in doing so, he would accept a written offer.

The book value of Ward Aero, Inc. had substantially increased since the merger, so I felt that it might be possible to start negotiations with an offer to purchase it at book value. I would also accept the liabilities as well as assets that included the substantial core charge fund. The only problem was that I did not wish to tie up our personal financial assets beyond those of the company and suggested that I would make the purchase for book value with nothing down and a

10-year payoff at some agreed upon interest. Medalist accepted this offer and we were on our way.

Though the Merlin II propjet was on our books, I did not need an asset of that worth. When I brought this up during negotiations to Mr. Fisher, he said that he had already figured on taking that over and wanted to move it to Milwaukee in a hangar that just became available to purchase. He felt that I could train one of his office personnel to handle the scheduling and related issues.

I decided to take on a couple of minority shareholders to provide operating capital. These were a local dentist and a retired lawyer and their wives. They proved to be true friends indeed. When I decided to sell Ward Aero, Inc. in 1977 they were both apparently satisfied with their return on investment and did not stand in the way of a pending transaction. Things like this can get sticky and hold up a deal but that was not to be the case. They remain friends to this day.

My final 26 year involvement with Ward Aero, Inc. came after a 26-year history during late 1977, when I was paid a personal visit from Herb Katz, President of the Airborne Division of Parker Hannifin Company, and his General Manager, Bill Seidel. During lunch, Herb and Bill queried as to what my plans for the future might be. I suggested that I was grooming the company and gearing up my life to sell at the age of fifty-five. I was then only fifty. The abbreviated version is that they traveled from Ohio to Three Rivers to buy lunch and make an offer to purchase Ward Aero. I listened to the offer and told Herb that I needed a little time to study out his proposal by suggesting that about a minute and a half would be adequate time. Once again, an opportunity came our way and my decision proved to be rewarding. New adventures were soon to come. For several years, I had already started doing some outside consulting projects under the business name of "Forward Horizons," so an immediate transition into this extremely interesting and successful new world of consulting and other endeavors were just around the corner.

Never hire a person for a responsible position who has a visible ornament protruding through their tongue, lip, or eyebrow. Equally important – if they are a male, check to see if they have a shirt pocket. If so, is it equipped with a pen or pencil for taking notes? If not, you are asking for trouble. That individual has a complex and even worse, trusts their memory far too much.

By: Author

CHAPTER VII
HOW ROTARY INTERNATIONAL
CHANGED MY LIFE

The year was 1957 when I was destined to discover a completely foreign world of experience that came through the influence of one Dr. Peterson, a Podiatrist in our community and person I barely knew, when <u>Rotary International</u> entered my life. I was subsequently invited to join our local Rotary Club. This organization would forever help change my perspective on life and knit the fabric of my adult being from that year forward. Part of this story jumps ahead to a period after selling Ward Aero, Inc., but the chain started with this link to Rotary.

In those hardworking early business years, while I didn't realize it at the time, those one and a half hour weekly noon meetings forced me to veer off of my self-imposed killer work schedule. What is more, my complete personal and business life had revolved around aviators and the aviation industry. That's all I knew and frankly it was all that I thought I wanted to know. For the most part, the guys sitting around me couldn't have cared less about my chosen field of aviation. They primarily spoke about a wide range of events in their own business and personal lives. Without understanding it at the time, my own personal knowledge base became broadened, to say nothing of my communication and civic involvement skills. At a point in time during the mid 1960's, I was honored to become the President of our Three Rivers, Michigan 100 member Rotary Club.

It was hard work but a rewarding experience. I feel I did a good job, and worked with gusto to make each meeting very meaningful to those attendees. With tongue in cheek I likened it to having a baby once a week. I often state in jest that we Rotarians are a "meat and belch club with one foot in the grave and the other foot in the gravy." Believe me! It is much more than that. Though the following comments relate to Rotary International, they could very well apply to any community service club, such as Lions, Kiwanis, and other fine organizations.

Rotary is fun! Having been a Rotarian for over 48 years (with perfect attendance for a like period), it has been an honor to associate with community leaders both local and throughout the world.

I can assure you that my member friends at the Three Rivers, Michigan USA Rotary Club had never heard of the aviation mechanic school that I attended. Our club used to have an annual Michigan/ Michigan State football day. We were supposed to arrive at Rotary at the appointed time, and then sit at a table that displayed either a Michigan or Michigan State flag. You took your pick, depending upon whom you were rooting for on the next weekend game. I went along with this, but it used to bug me. Next to having a stick poked in my eye, I couldn't think of anything I'd rather do than root for either one. I confronted the problem one year in the late 1950's by fabricating my own very large flag painted with the name "Pittsburgh Institute Of Aeronautics". At the dining hall where we met for Rotary, I brought in my flag along with a folding card table. I then set up my "PIA" table in a remote corner of the building and not saying a word to anyone, dined all by myself. When it came time for the good natured jesting between the two university rivals by the members, I got my licks in about demanding equal time for my beloved PIA. The flags at the tables are no longer displayed during the Michigan-Michigan State game, but the Rotary members still go through the ritual of paying heavy fines to the Rotary coffers, if they are on the loosing team. To this day, I still get my licks in by rising on my feet and demanding in a loud voice to the President that the Pittsburgh Institute Of Aeronautics should get equal time and recognition while this frivolity is going on. The younger members sit there like dummies, not knowing what's going on, but the old timers still snicker as they remember me sitting alone at that card table. Our inside joke still provides me with an annual delight.

<u>Rotary is dedication!</u> I was honored when invited to join Rotary and attend the weekly noon meetings during my early years in business. This was when I was literally working seven days a week with fifteen-hour days just to survive. Those reading this who ever started a business will understand this dilemma. I guess youthful stamina makes this a physical possibility. I will never forget the day I was inducted into our club, when after the meeting, I made an off hand comment to one of the members, Dr. Jim Malcolm. It was along the lines of "How can I possibly do this, with the work schedule I have?" With no hesitation whatsoever, Jim shot back with "You're absolutely right! If you can't hack it, you should quit right now." One of Rotary's strengths is their attendance requirement. If one can't make over 65% of the meetings, you are out! This is not as difficult as it may sound due to the fact that there are clubs all over the world, and by attending two weeks ahead or two weeks after the home club meeting day, an official "make-up" can be secured. There is no doubt in my mind that Jim's no nonsense and very firm statement to me contributed to my being a 100% attendance member for all of these years. In my mind, I probably thought – "I'll show you," and I did! Can there be some sort of a map of one's destiny that causes his actions to go one way or the other? Perhaps so!

<u>Rotary instills ethics!</u> The Rotary *"4 Way Test"* has been around since I can remember. It goes like this:

In your personal and business life, apply these questions to the things we think, say, or do.
1. Is it the TRUTH?
2. Is it FAIR to all concerned?
3. Will it build GOOD WILL and BETTER FRIENDSHIP?
4. Is it BENEFICIAL to all concerned?

These simple words are profound in their own meaning. They can and have changed lives for the better across the globe.

On a humorous note I will always remember visiting with a Sturgis, Michigan Rotarian by the name of Loren Felt. Loren owned a used car lot and I was in the market for an inexpensive car. During the process of picking one off of the lot, it all came down to negotiating the bottom-line price. I will not take a back seat to anyone in my ability to negotiate, but during the procedure, when we were close to striking the deal, Loren stopped, led me out of his office and suggested that we continue our contest out in the hallway. When I queried him as to the purpose of this maneuver, he stated in emphatic terms, that he simply could not continue with negotiations in his office, with the framed Rotary 4 Way Test hanging on his wall.

Fair enough! As Rotarians, we both applied the test and to this day, I can't figure out whether we both passed or failed the test. At any rate, I got a decent car for a decent price and hopefully Loren was able to make a few bucks. Right after that incident, I invoked rule number 5 and in jest at our next Rotary chapter meeting told this story then demanded that our local Rotary adapt a 5th test. It is:

5. Is it a GOOD DEAL?

Oh yes! Loren decided to go back to college and become a lawyer. I hope for the sake of his clients that he took his framed Rotary 4 Way Test with him into his law office.

<u>Rotary improves the world!</u> None of the following would ever have occurred without my involvement in Rotary International. This example will demonstrate power of the far reaching and influence of such an organization. In September of 1986, I received a call from a good friend and business associate – Dick Wagner of the Wagner Foundation. Dick's opening remark was, "What have you done for humanity lately?" It seems that he and his wife Bobbie, had worked with the Rotary Club of Burlington, Wisconsin in a major fundraising effort. They secured an ambulance airplane to donate for humanitarian use to the small Central American democracy of Belize. The aircraft of choice was a Cessna 206 complete with a Rotary emblem on the tail. It had already been secured, and outfitted with a stretcher-configured interior by "Wings Of Hope," a humanitarian aviation organization based in St. Louis. All they needed was for someone to get the operation moving through a coordinated effort with the Belize Ministry Of Health. I soon discovered the mission would be to fly in and out of the jungle almost every day for three months conducting medical missions for the Belize City Hospital. Saying no to Dick Wagner was not an option

so in a few days off I went with my faithful wife Donna by my side. We based the airplane and launched our flights from the small airport strip in San Pedro Town, located on Ambergris Caye. Our living quarters consisted of one room with a bed with foam rubber for a mattress, small sink, a two-burner stove, a privy and even an antique bathtub. This multifunction facility doubled as the spare parts room for the aircraft, and smelled like rubber tires during the whole period. Donna cried that first night! For me, it was all part of the game. For her, "culture shock" would be a gross understatement. To her credit though, she soon got right into the swing of things by manning the two-meter short wave radio. These were our lines of communication. The Belize hospital would radio to the Paradise Hotel, since they had a high antenna there, and Paradise would radio us with details for the flight. We both carried our two-meter Icom radios with us night and day. This crude communication technique would work amazingly well, but certainly needed improvement. Donna picked up all kinds of tricks. How do you wash your clothes? No problem! Soap them down and stomp on them with your bare feet in the bathtub. I'm certain that you get the idea and my Donna was up for the challenge.

I took the intensity of the sunup to sundown flying humanity missions pretty well in stride, but it was intense from time to time. Here are a couple of examples.

Flying in the country was not permitted at night. The only runway lights were at the International Airport in Belize City. A couple of times this issue became a life and death matter. On one such occasion, a knock on our door occurred at about 1:00 AM. Dr. Rodriguez, the local Clinic doctor, said that there were two fellows who had been stabbed and must be transported or they would die from loss of blood. The attempt to tell him that we were restricted from night flying met with deaf ears. He simply said, "Let's get going!" Within minutes I was at the airplane and they carried the patients to us from the Clinic on a wide wooden board. Apparently someone had borrowed the clinic stretcher. With efficiency, Dr. Rodriguez brought along a sheet of plastic. Spreading it on the floor of the aircraft was a prudent thing to do. I shouted to Donna to call the British Defense Force at the airport on the mainland and alert them as to what I was doing and make certain that they turned on the runway lights where we were to land. With that, along with the doctor and two bleeding guys in the cabin, I launched the 206 from the bonds of earth using our landing lights to line up on the dirt strip for takeoff. Checking flying weather in Belize at that time was impossible. No one manned the tower after dark. The 15-minute trip over the ocean was commingled with silence broken only in my mind; I am sure by some words of silent prayer that I must have been uttering. There was a navigational aid in the form of a VOR adjacent to the field. It was still operational and with that I was able to make an instrument approach into the fairly low ceiling. Unfortunately, the BDF did not take the hint to turn on the lights, but I was able to secure a visual reference by noting a large unlighted area in front of me where the airport should have been. Indeed, it was, and with my landing lights on, the pavement on the main runway came up under the nose of the airplane. Amen! By the way, both guys lived.

In another incident, as I was walking from our apartment to attend a Lions Club meeting where I was to explain the Wings Of Hope mission, I realized as I was almost there that I had neglected to grab my radio. This object was a lifeline used in our operation simply had to be clipped to my side at all times, so in a modest run I retraced my steps. When about half way back I heard a shrill scream immediately followed by a woman running out the open door of her house. I discovered that her small daughter had attempted to light their gas oven and it exploded in her face, moving her frail body against a wall in the process. It was not a pretty sight.

Knowing that Dr. Rodriguez from the Lions Clinic was not on the Island that day, I made a decision to place the girl into the Cessna and transport her over to Belize City. Everything fell into place. There was a driver in a pickup truck that I had already stopped to assist and we carefully placed the girl on a blanket in the bed of the truck and transported her to the aircraft, which was parked on the landing strip a few blocks away. Going by, I spotted Donna and had her radio the hospital to have them dispatch an ambulance to the landing strip near the Belize City Hospital. I have no idea how this was accomplished in the time that it was, but the complete process from the time I heard the scream including ground transport and the takeoff and landing amounted to something around a half hour. The Cessna 206 flies well at full throttle and 500 feet over the ocean.

Knowing full well that the Lions meeting would be started on "Belize time" (meaning that nothing ever starts on time), I was able to return and make my speaking engagement to the locals. The Lions members were impressed and became supportive and appreciative of the Wings Of Hope mission. By the way, I was able to follow the young girl's progress and with the exception of some modest scarring which was only slightly noticeable, she came out just fine.

Had I not forgotten my 2-way radio and gone back at that very moment, the results would have been completely different. Donna called the complete episode "Divine intervention." Who can argue? There were many other emergencies too numerous to mention.

Only four days were available for relaxation during the three-month period. There I was, an avid SCUBA diver, flying over the world's second longest barrier reef, with no time to view those marvelous underwater sights. That would have to come later, and it did. The airplane availability was paramount so I was able to hone my mechanical skills from time to time, with the valuable assistance of Wayne Casselberry, an American living in Belize. Wayne unselfishly made himself available at any hour of the day or night to lend a hand to keep our bird mechanically happy.

If there would be a way to have people in the Western World experience the austerity of a developing nation as part of their education, it would be a humbling and positive experience. A simple thing such as a paper clip becomes a tool that is taken very seriously when deprived of one. This was soon driven home to me when I took one of my first emergency trips to Punta Gorda, Belize. This town on the southern part of the country was 45 minutes from the Belize City hospital in our Cessna 206, but eleven hours by ground vehicle. That is assuming that the streams were not flooded. When taxiing in to pick up the patient who was being transported on the floor of the back end of a jeep, a number of us lifted him out and transferred him on to the aircraft's litter, by grasping a bed sheet he was laying on. Secured by belts on his stretcher, I fired up the engine, preparing to takeoff, when the fellow driving the jeep waved me down. It seems that I had started to run off with one of his valuable possessions, namely the bed sheet the patient was on. After that episode, I imposed on a friend who worked at the Paradise Hotel to make a midnight clothesline raid and make a donation of one bed sheet to Wings Of Hope. With my spare sheet as now part of my flight gear, I had the elements of an exchange program, and used it quite frequently during future flights.

Then there was the episode at the Belize City Hospital during our first visit. Not wanting to risk the perils of bad water, I always carried a flask of boiled water with me. I simply could not risk getting ill. The office of the Hospital Administrator was up an outside stairway. Directly inside was a modest reception desk with the Administrator's assistant positioned adjacent to his office. As I entered, I spotted a typical inverted large bottled water-dispensing machine with a spigot. Several small paper cups were stacked neatly upside down adjacent to the spigot. Wishing to save my own ration of water for use throughout the day, I queried as to whether she would mind if I took a drink from the bottle of water. "Certainly," was her immediate reply. Upon completion, I looked for a wastebasket. Seeing none, I asked the lady if she had a wastebasket behind her desk. She promptly advised me that these cups were not discarded but rather, should be placed back on the stack! I obliged in amazement and for an instant, pictured my many summer visits as a kid using the ever-present community tin cup that hung by the kitchen well pump handle in Grandma Ward's Tennessee farm home. The circle was complete.

It was no small task, but fate allowed me to keep my Rotary attendance record intact by attending the Belize City Rotary Club during their regular meetings. I came and went in my flight suit but they did not seem to mind.

After 3 months, we turned the established Wings Of Hope flight operation over to a permanent pilot and returned home. Donna and I took the communication problems we encountered in Belize very personally, and after returning made the local area speaking circuit to urge our friends and associates to pitch in to a fund so we could purchase a network of 2-meter radios and place them with the clinics and police of each town serviced by a landing strip throughout Belize. We also decided to place a radio base station with antenna tower at the main Belize City Hospital as well as at the landing strip at San Pedro, where the airplane was based. Over USD $13,000 was raised for the project and the radios were shipped off.

No one actually knew when the main hospital in Belize City was constructed on the ocean's edge. The nails holding the boards together were so rusted that they had lost their effectiveness. The operating room table had a rust hole through it from corrosion and cardboard covering the hole. A tour through the kitchen revealed no hot water and a stove with a ventilation hood over it, with the top of the hood leading back into the room. Basic supplies were always in short supply. In short, you would not want to become sick and have to go to the Belize City Hospital during those days. As fate would dictate, right after returning we discovered a real bonanza right in our own back yard. Our hometown of Three Rivers, Michigan constructed a brand new hospital and equipped it with virtually all new equipment. Could we get all of the old but still excellent equipment and donate it to our Belize Minister Of Health? We could and we did. Our local Hospital Board gave us an affirmative nod and it was ours. Working through my local Rotary Club and coordinating the receiving of the materials with the Belize City Rotary Club, we took this on as a project. Equally important our club worked with the local Lions Club in getting the job done. They took on the massive hands on job of crating all of this equipment so it could be properly shipped. How to get it there became a challenge that I took on personally, by working through some key people at the Air National Guard. After much coaxing, I received an OK from the Air Force Reserve in Detroit, and was able to use two military C-130 cargo aircraft to deliver the goods. This was done as in a most efficient manner and was flight logged as one of their navigational training missions. Hell's bells, you've got to train somewhere! Civilians were not permitted on this mission but I got around this through my credentials as a freelance writer, and was granted a crew clearance. On a clear sunny day, in mid-November of 1988, both C-130's landed with over $400,000 USD worth of supplies and equipment for the hospital. As we taxied in, a brass band literally met us along with the Ambassador, Minister of Health and other dignitaries. I accepted a plaque during that ceremony on behalf of all of the people back home that pulled this off. Later on, the country of Belize constructed a brand new hospital where much of this equipment is currently seeing service. This plaque, improperly recognizing me as an individual when it was such a group effort, hangs prominently on my office wall as a constant reminder of this event. A CBS affiliate reporter and photographer went along and later produced a documentary that was aired on television.

ACCEPTING AWARD OF APPRECIATION FROM BELIZE
GOVERNMENT OFFICIAL
R. Ward Collection

Rotary is action! If all of that wasn't enough, after returning to the States, our Rotary District 6360 office heard about the projects going on between Belize and Three Rivers, and Karl Sandelin, the then District Governor, visited with me. He informed me that the District 6360 wanted to take on an international project with Belize. Ultimately it took on the following format. Each of our District Rotary Clubs would adapt an individual school in the country and be responsible for giving it a hand. Pages could be devoted to detail this effort but suffice to say that it was successful beyond belief. The project was tagged "Belizerve" and hit the mark by changing the face of education in this small country. The school Three Rivers adapted was in the town of Libertad in the District of Corozal. Juana Terry, the School Principal worked with us through the Corozal Rotary Club, and brought her school from the lowest position in education to the number one school in the country. Tons of educational books and supplies made their way to Belize. They were transported by sea in shipboard containers and more literally driven in many donated vehicles such as donated school busses and ambulances. Going there at their own expense, many Rotarians went with hammer and saw in hand to assist the villagers in construction of new facilities, and lasting international friends were developed. Today, the Libertad RC School is the crown jewel of this small community. They are even equipped with a state of the art computer, and are online with the rest of the world.

Rotary accelerates positive change! To point out this one example, tremendous change has occurred in Belize since that short time ago. It was then critically in need for basic things as we know it but yet was truly an orchid in the swamp. Tourists from everywhere have since discovered this poor but democratic English speaking country with its friendly people. It is thriving as a world-class vacation destination. Wings Of Hope is still alive and well working with the Ministry Of Health in their Humanitarian flight missions. The Wagner Foundation continues assisting in their unselfish manner in ways known by few. They have been responsible for the establishment of a countrywide EMT program, as one example, and the Belize health system is proudly up and running. Though our Rotary District 6360 school program had a predetermined time limit when it started, many of the clubs within the district have continued with their one on one programs and will continue to do so.

Rotary is each individual! Could this chain of events have occurred and developed in such a manner without my receiving that single phone call in 1986 from my friend Dick Wagner? I don't think so! In the final analysis, we as individuals can do little to weave the threads of destiny, without the guiding hands of our supreme navigator. How else could it be?

Rotary is loyalty! As for me, I plan on attending Rotary for a while longer, meeting and belching with one foot in the grave, and the other foot in the gravy, until I run out of gravy, or until they fine

106

me for my last buck, whichever comes first. The way our club fines their members at each meeting, it may be my money but one thing is for certain. I plan on setting the record for Rotary International's all time perfect attendance. When I get to 100 years, I'm going to break the attendance chain, just for the heck of it.

CHAPTER VIII
A NEW WORLD OF ACTIVITIES

My routine changed dramatically when I was able to swing into my Forward Horizons consulting activities almost immediately. While entering into a new field quite by accident a friend asked me to go into partnership with him in some real estate investments. This developed into more than I ever thought would occur with a number of structures being constructed on leasebacks. They proved to be educational, interesting and quite profitable. While this was going on, I still found time to wade into several pro-bono activities in addition to my beloved Rotary Club. These provided me with a great amount of satisfaction as a means of paying others back for my good fortune, and continue to do so today.

The Beechcraft Twin Bonanza became my aircraft of choice for transportation, which to this day provides me with a huge dose of personal fulfillment. This continuity enabled me to stay in contact with my many aviation friends. Immediately after selling the business, there was an instant void in my life, because the company aircraft was no longer at my beck and call since I no longer owned the company and this perk. I had always owned an airplane; from the time I was 15 years old when I purchased my very first aircraft for just thirty-five dollars. One exception to this was when, during W.W.II, Uncle Sam supplied a Navy PBM Patrol Bomber at no charge. Life without an airplane for the first time was out of the question, and it became quite obvious that another aircraft had to be selected which would fulfill our transportation needs. Here is how this evolved.

The flight operation we had with our company Merlin II propjet during our affiliation with Medalist Industries was exceptional, but to consider ownership of this class machine on a personal level made little sense both from a practical and cost standpoint. It was time to scale down. As an aside, few are aware that all of the early Merlin II aircraft were literally constructed from components of the Beechcraft Twin Bonanza by Ed Swearingen of Swearingen Aircraft in San Antonio, Texas. The pressurized fuselage was of course a new design, but much of the airframe structure including wings, controls, landing gear, and electric motors were originally manufactured using Twin Bonanza parts.

The more I studied the market availability of used aircraft for my own transportation, the more obvious it became that the Twin Bonanza was a good candidate. Here are some of my personal reasons:

1. The aircraft was a limited edition by Beech and was already becoming a marketplace "Classic." Value would continue to increase.

2. The structural integrity was second to none, since it was originally designed with the military in mind.

3. The Lycoming GO-480 engine versions had a reasonable time between overhaul (1,400 Hrs.) and overhaul costs were reasonable.

4. Parts availability was not a major problem. Many parts are still available through the Beech Factory. Also, there are a number of surplus and salvage yard inventories to draw upon.

5. A radar nose and airstair dropdown steps to enter and exit the airplane a must for my own requirements. These were an original option on certain models of the Twin Bonanza and the Excalibur conversions.

6. Creature comforts abound. Elbow room, legroom, and headroom... or even get up and stretch. A great feature for long trips.

7. The older I get, the more assistance I like in the cockpit. The Twin Bonanza is no doubt the most stable instrument platform I had ever flown. Just think! No cowl flaps to worry about, and the

fuel systems are altitude compensated. That means no playing with mixture controls. Leave them in the rich position all of the time. Simply push the power levers and go.

With all of these advantages, there was a tradeoff. That tradeoff to a small degree was speed. The way the normally aspirated Twin Bonanza is usually operated, it is pretty much a 160-knot flying machine that burns about 29 gallons per hour (GPH) of fuel. Will it go faster? Of course! But you naturally burn more fuel and pay the piper. What most operators discover is that a compromised speed is a small price to pay in the overall scheme of things. The aircraft is so comfortable; the speed deficiency becomes quite a secondary matter. Another option was to search out an "Excalibur 800" conversion. Powered with two 400 HP Lycoming IO-720 engines there were only a handful of these made. That assumed of course that one of these limited edition models was available in the marketplace, which at the time was not an option. So, my own preliminary choice was made - a normally aspirated Twin Bonanza. The next step was to find the right used aircraft. When all was said and done, I ended up with a different technique than my original plan of securing an airworthy airplane. After hearing back from my mailing, I went to look over a rather sad looking model D50 sitting on the ramp in Richmond, Virginia. Looking at the logistics of doing so, I was prompted to take this unairworthy aircraft and conduct a total restoration. This particular machine had a blown engine, crazed glass, and flat struts/ tires and had literally been rain soaked on the inside from a window crack. Most people would have walked right by it and never given it a second look. It did however have the basic elements I was interested in. These included the Swearingen conversion of the airstair door, radar nose and enclosed landing gear doors. Most electronics were not that great, but for all practical purposes it all worked. The radios however, were eventually upgraded.

The end result was a full-blown restoration that made this aircraft practically new in function and appearance. To this day, it still looks and flies that way. As a matter of fact, it received an award during the 1993 Oshkosh Air show for the most "Outstanding Custom Multi-Engine" aircraft. I operated N12FH for 20 years when in 1998, I found and reconstructed our beautiful Excalibur 800 that serves us well to this day. Captain Jack Clary proudly parks N12FH in the hangar that is an integral part of his home at Spruce Creek, a fly-in community near Daytona Beach, Florida. It's in good hands and that gives me a good feeling.

D50 N12FH & D50C EXCALIBUR 800 NOSE TO NOSE
Note long flat cowling housing the 400 HP 8 cylinder engines on
N800EX
R. Ward Collection

It became clear as soon as I secured our Beechcraft Twin Bonanza (also affectionately called the "T-Bone" or "Twinbo") that it was becoming a classic aircraft, because of its rich heritage and military background. While my reconstruction of N12FH was taking place in Richmond Virginia, I met another T-Bone owner, one Dr. Jim Seymour, who was having his aircraft inspected at the same facility that I had contracted to do my work. Dr. Seymour still pilots his same aircraft today, after these many years. We both agreed that sometime in the near future there should be an association formed to chronicle the attributes and history of the Twin Bonanza and network with other proud owners, historians and aficionados. We would call it the "Twin Bonanza Association (TBA)." I finally agreed to take on the task, knowing full well that it would eat up a vast quantity of my spare time, but made it quite clear that I would accept the challenge only with the complete understanding that I would run the TBA much like Hitler ran Germany. We would not vote, nor would we have any committees. The major difference though was that if anyone complained or thought they could do a better job, I would ship them everything and they could take over. To date, if there are any complaints, they must be taking place behind my back, since I have not yet made that shipment. The TBA website <u>www.twinbonanza.com</u> can be viewed in case you wish to learn more.

DICK & DONNA WARD BY THEIR
EXCALIBUR 800 D50C N800EX
R. Ward Collection

My experiences operating the Beechcraft Twin Bonanza Association for over 20 years brings many thoughts to mind, most of which have added significant aroma to the spice of life. I publish a Newsletter each quarter and we have an annual "Gathering Of The Bones" where we meet for several days and enjoy each other's company. The friends we have met and retained through the years are a treasure for Donna and myself.

I get many phone calls, as you might imagine, relating to techniques as well as mechanical questions. Many of them are from persons who are not TBA members, but that's OK. I do encourage them to join our group, and most often they eventually do so. This one person however, let's call him Dilbert, (shades of my Navy Air Corps days) kept calling me, without exaggeration, at least a dozen times asking for advise about several T-Bones he was considering for purchase. You guessed it, most of them were parked in some remote location with questionable engines and oh yes, just "light" corrosion on some of the control surfaces.

I have this basic theory that I pass along from time to time. It is: 'Youz pays now or youz pays later.' Dilbert was quick to change the subject each time I gave him this recitation. Oh yes during each call he would remind me that he is going to join the TBA, as soon as he gets time to write a $35.00 check for his dues. To be sure, the check was already written for a copy of my book, but it was yet to be mailed and he wanted to do both together. Yea right! I don't have to work for food, but you can imagine that this scenario gets old pretty quick. Nevertheless, I will never shut off a person when I can be helpful, and that is that. My mission is to assist other "T-Boners."

Timed to perfection, at about 1830 EST, whilst enjoying one of Donna's home cooked meals the phone rang. Dilbert was on the other end with the enlightening news that he had just purchased an early model Twin Bonanza, but though flyable, it needed "some work." He sounded excited. The phone connection seemed very poor with noise and voices in the background. I suggested that he call me back on my other line to see if it would clear. He commented that he did not have too much time to chat, but if I could put up with the connection, he just had a couple of questions to ask. I told Dilbert to proceed.

The questions he asked related to power management. "Dick did you say that you pull back on the props before the throttles after takeoff or was it the other way around? What is a good cruise setting?" and those types of questions. I think I suggested that all of these questions and many more were answered in my Twin Bonanza book but I proceeded to give him a 5-minute verbal course anyhow.

The phone connection was getting more and more obscured. I continued hearing some speech in the background that sounded like radio chatter, and queried if he was sitting at an FBO. He came back with the comment that he had to cut our conversation short because <u>he had just been cleared for takeoff</u>. MY GAWD! Dilbert was apparently sitting at the end of the runway when he called.

I heard him repeat "Roger – cleared for takeoff". He said thanks to me and noted that he would give me another call when he arrived at his destination, which was Las Vegas. The phone connection, though hard to hear, was still open and as I continued to listen, I started to hear him conversing with some other person who apparently was in the right seat. I wish that I could have heard what they were saying, but the voices were muffled. Nevertheless the chattering continued. Dilbert must have laid his phone down and in his excitement forgot to terminate my call.

This was an opportunity too good to pass up, so I left my phone off the hook and finished my meal. About a half hour later the connection was still in place. When I checked in another hour or so, I could still hear muffled conversation. I'm not certain when I finally hung it up, but it was pretty dark outside.

I wonder where Dilbert is now? His TBA dues payment check apparently never made it through the mail. Maybe it got lost, but more likely; he had to use those funds to pay off his understandably large cell telephone invoice. Then there would still have been the cost of patching up some of the "light" corrosion on those control surfaces. 'Youz pays now or youz pays later,' Dilbert.

Twin Bonanza Association Logo
R. Ward Collection

Have you ever heard of SCORE? SCORE stands for the **S**ervice **C**orps **O**f **R**etired **E**xecutives, and is comprised of retired professionals who have been successful in their own business careers and are now in a position to help others while receiving no remuneration for doing so. When a retired businessperson from Kalamazoo, Michigan heard about me having sold my company, he paid a visit and explained how I might be helpful to others. In 1980 I joined SCORE and have been a member ever since.

It's nice to think that when you plant grass on your lawn that all you have to do is mow it once in a while and it will look good forever. To remain abundant however, some new grass seed must occasionally be planted in order to have the lawn really thrive. That, figuratively speaking is how the SCORE people think of their work. There comes a time in life when it simply gives one a good feeling to help replant some grass seed on the other person's lawn when your own is growing well. In the eyes of SCORE Counselors, that's the proper thing to do.

Who are these people? SCORE's volunteer counselors are all experienced and seasoned in their respective work related fields. These include: retailers, plant managers, sales managers, financial persons, and many more. In fact, there are exactly 50 such volunteers in the Kalamazoo Chapter alone. This Chapter covers an area of southwestern Lower Michigan. They stand by ready to share their know-how for those business associates currently in operation or to assist the rapidly growing legions of entrepreneurs ready to start their own business. SCORE members say, "The pay is excellent." Though there is never a charge made to those who use SCORE, and no money ever reaches the pockets of the counselors who provide this service, the reward comes in the satisfaction of seeing their clients succeed in business. Helping others...that's what SCORE is all about.

Does SCORE have a track record? Since being established in 1964, SCORE personnel throughout the United States have counseled thousands of small businesses. The call for help ranges from those starting up a new business to existing businesses needing specific expertise within certain areas. The size of the problems being faced by these owners is vastly different, but their goals are always the same – to see their business succeed. Sometimes SCORE will be contacted where only a miracle would help prevent the business from going under. Those are the tough ones. But... miracles occasionally come about (with a little help from SCORE).

How does one request this service? Simply request a SCORE counseling session by phone or mail. You will receive a simple form that should be returned to the SCORE office. The secretary will arrange for a skilled counselor to conduct an initial meeting and then follow through as required. Quite often a SCORE team technique may be used once the ball is rolling, when multiple talents might be useful.

Challenges abound! Whether helping develop a business plan, showing methods used in becoming organized, establishing a sales plan, or even sitting down and becoming a listening partner so that a problem can be placed into sharp focus before a decision for the fix is recommended. SCORE counselors thrive on facing the problem head on with their clients, and then assist the business entrepreneur in making a final decision.

There is a primary difference between a SCORE counselor and a paid business consultant, however. We act as advisors and leave the hands on work to the client. A paid consultant if called upon to do so would become a hands on person. A good example of this would be that you could hire a paid consultant to write a business plan for you. We would walk you through the process, and make you do it yourself. Then once complete, would critique what was accomplished.

For me personally, I get a good feeling to be able to assist budding entrepreneurs and share some of the lessons I have learned along the way in an effort to have them succeed. I have success stories and also many failures with clients I have advised, as one might imagine. Each of our SCORE counselors is different in their skills so we try to mesh the client with those skills wherever possible.

I differ in principal in a couple of areas with many of my SCORE associates. The first relates to start up money. Often we meet with a client who has virtually no money to get his/her business started. Some of our counselors feel they are doing them a favor by telling them that there is absolutely no way that they can succeed because of this lack of capital. I simply refuse to do that. Rather, I will go into great detail to let them know what I believe their odds for success might be. Before doing so however, I try to seek out how much they are willing to sacrifice. Are they, for example, willing to work the fifteen-hour days, seven days a week and three hundred sixty-five days per year to give things a try? Then comes the $64,000 question. Is your spouse prepared to go along with this? If the answers to these questions are yes, there is a possibility that one may succeed. To my way of thinking, moving forward with the right attitude makes up for a huge amount of front-end capital. How do I know? It worked for me and I see it in others, that's how. I believe that everyone has the right to succeed, but they also have the right to fail and try again. The key to success is to work at what you love to do. Notice that I said *work* at what you do, not *play* at what you do.

Count those souls in the setting sun that run
their business for cost and fun

By: Author

Then there is the all important (to some people) "Mission Statement." Garbage! The mission in business is simple. Work your butt off and make your business succeed so that you can be proud and perhaps even accumulate a little wealth while you're having fun. This trendy thing can be seen everywhere. They hang on walls, are proudly displayed in advertisements and even used for handouts. Ask virtually any employee what their company mission statement is and I'll betcha 2 to 1 that they can't recite it.

Those who work for money alone will not find happiness. Work hard at what you love to do and money will always come.

By: Author

My chance to serve our government was personally rewarding. While I won't dwell on all of the details, I hasten to mention in 1982, an opening occurred in the Michigan House of Representatives that got my attention for several reasons. Being a conservative Republican, I felt that it was time for a businessman to step up to the plate and impose a ration of common sense into the State House. The candidate who was already making a play for the open position had run a couple of times previously and lost, and it appeared to me that he was not at all the conservative Representative I wanted working for me in Lansing. Immersing oneself into a race of this type is a noble experiment that I recommend for anyone who feels they should do their part, instead of simply whining to others. Donna, trooper that she is said, "Go for it." Not wishing to be tainted by others with an agenda, we did not solicit funds and spent $17,000 of our own money. Parades, debates, direct mail, and knocking on doors were all part of the political marketing plan. My well-publicized plank included the fact that I would do everything within my power to establish term limits so the politicians would not become ingrained within the system. The end result was I lost that election by a slim margin. My opponent, having run and lost previously, had the name recognition that pushed him into the job. To my delight, term limits finally became a reality in Michigan and a conservative Representative who is willing to lay it on the line with his liberal counterparts has since been elected.

Ward brochure cover used in election
R. Ward Collection

There are the givers and there are the takers – If you are only one without the other, a satisfied life will pass you by. Where does your life fit?

By: Author

CHAPTER IX
FLYING TALES

COMPANY FLYING – SOME INTERESTING TWISTS

The Kirsch Company, manufacturers of drapery hardware, was a family run organization in Sturgis, Michigan that operated a twin-engine company aircraft as far back as the 1940's. After we moved to Three Rivers in 1952, the Chief Pilot discovered that I was twin-engine rated and asked if I would consider checking out in their DeHavilland Dove as a Captain. Kirsch operated a pilot/copilot operation at that time and when one of them wanted off for a few days, I could then do some fill in flying for them. The Chief Pilot whom I prefer not to name was well skilled in the cockpit but was not without his faults. When flying with him, he would continually peck-peck-peck at meaningless things. This got old pretty fast with me. When I put him in his place it got better for me but never for his regular copilot. Another observation is he would never hire a copilot that was skilled enough to be able to take over his job. I guess he figured that it was job protection. Nor would he ever let them fly a full leg of a trip. I worked with one of his copilots, Wilbur Hente, to the point he was able to pass his checkride for an instrument rating, using my Beechcraft Bonanza. When I flew with Wilbur in the Dove, I would always let him fly one leg of the trip then I would fly the other. This kept us both sharp, but neither of us ever made a point of touting this to the Chief Pilot, because it could have placed Wilbur in jeopardy.

As an aside, the Kirsch family always treated their people with dignity and respect. On our many trips to Pompano Beach, Florida, where they had a winter home it was not unusual for them to put us up in a beachside resort and take us to dinner or out on their yacht.

During those days some pilots were on the make by taking gifts disguised in many forms, and making undocumented deals with vendors. It was not unusual for this particular Chief Pilot to be able to rent an aircraft from one large Fixed Base Operator who did the maintenance on the Kirsch aircraft for a little getaway to Florida and then "forget" to send him an invoice. Things like that were constantly going on in some circles but I would never play their game.

Later Kirsch purchased a G-18 Twin Beech, then a short time later a Howard 500 Lockheed, This guy finally got his just deserts when Kirsch Company decided to enter into the jet world and authorized him to study things out and acquire a different airplane. He selected a Jet Commander for reasons soon to become evident. This choice made no sense whatsoever because the early versions had limited fuel range. Keep in mind that the Florida trips were scheduled quite often and that damn thing would require a fuel stop. So much for speed!

As told to me by the Kirsch Company General Manager, when the actual aircraft purchase transaction took place in Mr. Kirsch's office, the aircraft salesman, and the Kirsch Chief Pilot were present along with the company controller. When it came time to exchange the bills of sale for a payment check from the Kirsch controller, the swap was made. At this point the salesman turned to Mr. Kirsch and said: "One last thing! Here is my certified check back to you for the kickback that your Chief Pilot demanded." With that he handed him the check and left the room.

I don't know how long it took, but it must have been less than a day, since that particular Chief Pilot almost immediately left the community for parts unknown and to this day, no one I know has ever heard from him. I did hear that shortly after the incident that he started selling asphalt, however. Remember the "Hog" theory?

Richard I. Ward

*My daddy told me he ain't never seen a hog die
a natural death.*

By: Author

SOMETIMES OUR FEET SHOULD BE USED FOR MORE THAN WALKING!

During the early part of 1955 and at the request of an old friend by the name of Max Karant whom was then head of the Aircraft Owners and Pilots Association (AOPA), called to see if I could give them some assistance. He requested that I volunteer the (free) use of my Instructor capabilities as well as my 1947 model 35 Bonanza to partake in a developmental program that the AOPA Foundation started. They were working with Dr. Leslie Bryan through the Institute of Aviation at the University of Illinois. He also thought it would be helpful to see if someone from my local CAA office would ride along. I was assured that it would only involve a few days of my time, and I was further assured that the trip would be interesting and enlightening. That statement proved to be a gross understatement. One of the good guys of those days in my neighborhood was a CAA Flight Operations man out of South Bend, Indiana by the name of Les Cooling. Les agreed to accompany me on this adventure. Here's what it was all about.

Those were the days when there was absolutely no instructional requirement for private pilots to expose themselves to any instrument training. That was considered advanced training in which most did not engage. This lack of training resulted in an atrocious number of weather related fatalities. The ground was harshly kissed all too often after the occupants experienced the deadly "graveyard spiral." It became obvious to AOPA that some basic training at that time, on a voluntary basis, should be promoted." This training was promoted as the "AOPA 180 degree Rating."

The goal of this course, after it was designed was the essence of simplicity. It only had to teach the pilot to keep the plane upright if unexpectedly encountering instrument weather conditions make a good enough 180 degree turn to get back to Visual Flight Rules

(VFR) weather, or to get down safely through a cloud deck. The plan had to be inexpensive and practical and adaptable to all single engine aircraft currently flying. This even included the old Cubs, Champs, Chiefs, and T-Crafts. Before the course could be actually designed, it was deemed prudent to study the problem in the real world. This is where myself, Les Cooling, and a contingent of other interested aviators came in, working with the University of Illinois flight team. We used our aircraft and instructional talents to fly with a number of nonprofessional pilots, placing them under simulated instrument conditions at strategic times, and then to record the event. By the way, we simulated instrument conditions by outfitting our aircraft and clipping amber Plexiglas on the inside of the windshield and all windows, and having the pilot wear blue goggles. They saw well within the cockpit through the blue goggles but the outside view through the amber Plexiglas was black. The instructors of course wore no goggles and could see clearly through the windshield and windows. Fortunately I saved the report published by AOPA and am able to reconstruct the following facts with accuracy for you, referring to this manual.

The 20 subjects that were used were all Airplane Single Engine Land (ASEL) light plane pilots with an age range from 19 through 60. Total flight times ranged from 31 to 1,620 hours. Cross-country times ranged from 0 to 1,500 hours, Night-flying time from 0 to 50, BUT none had any instrument time. The aircraft selected for the experiment was the Model 35 Beech Bonanza, because it represented the most complex light single engine aircraft of its day and if the newly designed technique could be learned using this aircraft, it would work in virtually anything. That it did!

The purpose of the first flight period was to acquire some indication of the subject's ability to control the airplane under instrument conditions and to give the student a dramatic appraisal of his/her ability or lack thereof as an instrument pilot. During the flight, all of the subjects were shown the use of each instrument and allowed to practice without the goggles. The first simulated instrument flight was then started at 2500 MSL (1750 actual feet). This lower altitude was selected to magnify the apparent potential disaster as the ground was staring him in the face when the goggles were raised.

After the subject felt comfortable with the use of the instruments and had a chance to settle in a bit, the blue goggles were lowered. Then the fun began. Of the 20 subjects, nineteen placed the aircraft in a graveyard spiral and the 20th pulled the airplane up into a whipstall attitude which most certainly would have resulted in a rapid buildup of airspeed to a point of structural failure. The time to reach the impending dangerous altitude ranged from a minimum of 20 seconds to a maximum of eight minutes. The results were obvious. All occupants would have crashed and probably died.

During the exercise the speed was never allowed to exceed 200 mph and needless to say, the instructor blocked the elevator with a firm grip on the yoke as the goggles were lifted. Seeing the earth at such a low altitude looking them in the eye would naturally create the urge to pull back rapidly with inevitable structural failure following the pull. Sound familiar? Just read some of today's accident reports.

If you think there were not twenty humble pilots out there after going through this, you have another think coming. They were eager candidates to glean the next phase: learning the 180-degree training.

The technique was the essence of simplicity and primarily involved concentration on only one instrument, the TURN & BANK INDICATOR. These were readily available for a few bucks from any WWII surplus house along with a simple 2" venturi and could be installed in a short time in any kind of an aircraft not already equipped with one. Here is the way it worked. A safe yet moderate airspeed was selected for each aircraft make and model. On the Bonanza, this was designated to be 95 mph, with the landing gear down. The propeller control was placed in low pitch and flaps were not used. Once airspeed was established, the elevator trim tab position was marked on a piece of masking tape and taped alongside the trim indicator. A tape marker is then placed on the manifold pressure gauge at the setting that held 95 mph. On the Bonanza this amounted to about 17 inches. With a fixed pitch propeller aircraft, the marking would be on the tachometer, of course. These preliminary markings were critical to the concept. It lessened the burden of the pilot. Instead of having to remember numbers, he had only to make reference to the markings, in any future weather emergency.

During initial training great importance was placed on the Turn & Bank indicator and was treated as our very best friend. Beyond measuring the rate of turn with the needle, one has to appreciate the fact that as long as the needle is centered, there is no way that a graveyard spiral can occur. The student learned to average the needle with any right/left swings. The needle was controlled with the pilot's feet alone. They do all of the work. I already mentioned that the real killer was the elevator. Simply getting the student's hands completely off of the stick or wheel and leaving them off, during the complete operation, resolved that problem. The course consisted of 5 training periods with periods 3, 4, and 5 devoted to practice. So here's how it goes in an actual emergency. When entering instrument weather, the following steps are taken:

Center the turn needle with the rudder; keep it centered.

Hands Off the flight controls
Keep hands off the controls
Lower the landing gear.
Reduce the Power to somewhere above a high idle.
Roll the trim to its predetermined mark.
Adjust the propeller pitch to Low (High RPM).
Set power to the predetermined setting.

Note: During the foregoing operations, the aircraft will in all probability oscillate until its predetermined airspeed is reached. Any attempt to correct these oscillations manually would probably prove futile and could induce uncontrollable oscillations. <u>Keep hands off flight controls</u>.

Check the Compass Heading – Though it may be different than the original heading, an estimate of the reciprocal heading should be made, that lead him into the weather originally.

Turn with the rudder. Use no more than ¾ needle deflection during the turn. This provides a shallow bank. Remember that the needle controls the rate of the turn while the ball only tells us the quality of the turn. If the ball is in the cage, it is a coordinated turn, if it's not and the needle is still veered to one side or the other, the aircraft is still turning, though it may not be exactly coordinated. On that minor issue, in an emergency situation, who cares?

Roll out on the desired heading using lead or lag if relying on a magnetic compass or on heading if using a gyro.

Descending or climbing is accomplished by the deletion or addition of power. Typically a difference of 5 to 6 inches of manifold pressure or 300 to 500 rpm, in the case of a fixed pitch propeller.

Remember that hands never touch the flight control yoke until the aircraft is in safe VFR weather. All of the work is done with the rudder.

From time to time pilots should revisit the Turn & Bank indicator. It is a great friend that just sits in the corner presumably doing nothing. Nothing, that is, until all goes to Hell in a bushel basket and the artificial horizon goes belly up. We continue to read about our flying friends who somehow make the fatal plunge toward earth with normally operating engines. Just for the fun of it, you might even want to set your aircraft up to fly hands off as I've described. Set the power and trim to the mark and practice some maneuvers. It's amazing how precise the aircraft can be flown using only your feet.

Those reading this who do not have an instrument rating at the very least go set your airplanes up with the markings discussed and practice the techniques. After all of these years, I still believe that it has great merit, even though the FAA introduced technique differs dramatically.

As a final note, I went on to instruct the 180 AOPA 180 degree methods to many pilots, in all kinds of aircraft in the Michigan and Indiana areas. My guess is that a number of lives may have been saved in the forthcoming years.

TO FEATHER OR NOT TO FEATHER? THAT IS THE QUESTION

Should one feather the propeller when a problem is noted once a reasonable altitude is reached after take-off? Bring this question up around a hangar flying session at the airport some Saturday morning and you will get many opinions, though there is no pat answer. I generally concur with the idea of not feathering a prop while one is at altitude below the single engine service ceiling and the engine is still producing power. This assumes that there is no fire or mechanical damage risk, of course but each situation should obviously be evaluated.

My own experience as it relates to this dates back to the late 1950's when I was flying a Model G-18 Twin Beech back to Michigan from Pompano Beach, Florida. My copilot noticed that some oil was streaming over the top of the cowling on the starboard engine. Tallahassee was approximately 20 minutes away and seemed to be the likely candidate for putting down, so I powered back on the affected engine and took a heading toward there, all the while keeping a strong eye on the oil pressure and temperature gauges. They remained within the green but the amount of oil showing up over the wing increased the pucker factor, to be sure. To feather or not to feather that was the question. My decision not to feather, unless we spotted a change in the pressure and temperature proved to be the right one. Here's why! After landing, we pulled off on a taxiway, shut both engines down, and then requested a tug move us onto the FBO ramp. On arrival, we noted that the cowling and wing were bathed in oil, but it seemed to be coming from the propeller area. The propeller was pulled and lo and behold, the propeller shaft on the P&W R985 engine was cracked over 3/4 of the way around directly at the thrust nut portion. With only a short piece of propshaft metal holding things together, no doubt exists in my mind that if we would have feathered, the propeller would have said "Bye Bye." and taken off on its own flight. In fact, I later discovered that this identical thing happened to Bob Welch, an old friend of mine from Alpena, Michigan when he feathered his engine on a Twin Beech that related to the same defect. He said that he watched in horror as the propeller went out and over his flying machine, hopefully to be returned later by some considerate farmer.

The root of this particular problem, by the way, stemmed from the threads on the propeller shaft that positions the thrust nut becoming stressed because the apex of the threads at the bottom were sharp. An FAA Airworthiness Directive was later issued to correct this problem. If my memory serves me, the fix was to hand grind the base of all of the threads using dental floss and valve lapping compound.

When I look at the scud below, I am nothing
When I look at the clouds ahead, I am nothing
When I look at my passengers, I am nothing
When I look at my radar, I am disgusted

By: Author

OUTMANEUVERING THE BIRDS!

In a 2004 issue of AOPA Pilot magazine, their "Never Again" column contained an article entitled "A Run of Gulls." In short, it recapped the author's experience as he collided with a flight of sea gulls. This reminds all of us that we are highly outnumbered by these critters as we share the air. Mr. Gibbons, the author, points out the sequence of events that occurred, including the high priority he initially and continually gave by using evasive action maneuvering, during the incident. It severely damaged his Cessna 172. His course of action is completely understandable, and for all I know, could have been proper.

My theory however, and one that I have used for more years than you want to hear about, is to *stay the course and take no action whatsoever*. That's right! When I see a bird through the windscreen... I drive on and take no evasive action. I personally do this on the premise that the bird is a pretty good airman and does not wish to die any more than do I. Though not certain, I think birds can also hear pretty well, and for the most part, probably get the idea that there is another bigger and noisier bird headed in their direction. On that premise, I feel that my odds are far better to allow the birds to take the evasive action, while I stay the course. For me to do so, at least in my mind, creates a scenario where the birds become confused as to which direction to go.

Over the number of years, in which I have accumulated over 500 flight hours giving 30-minute rides in the Kalamazoo AirZoo's (www.airzoo.org) 1929 Ford Tri-motor, our flights rarely take us over a thousand feet. Most of them are over marshes and lakes well stocked with flying birds. It is rare not to see some along our flight path at various altitudes. First of all, fast maneuvering in this machine is not even an option, as the response time is certainly not spectacular. Many times I have personally seen how the birds seem to know that we're coming and don't hesitate to tuck and dive to get out of our way.

Have I ever had a bird strike? Yes, I've had two in over 60 years of flying, and both of them were in the dark of night. In that scenario, all bets are off.

So there, I've said the unthinkable. Accept or reject my theory as you wish. Just don't sue me if you accept my premise and still have a collision with a bird. Keep in mind that there is still a percentage of the bird population that is hard of hearing, has poor vision and/or just plain stupid.

AirZoo 1929 Ford Tri-motor Model 5-AT-C
N8419, S/N 58
R. Ward Collection

Captain Dick Ward prior to a flight in Ford Tri-motor N8419
R. Ward Collection

CHAPTER X
TOUCH AND GO

RAISING THE BOYS – I THINK WE DID OK!

DANE - While sifting recently through a box of school papers left behind in our home by our first son Dane, I was attracted to read an 8-page book report on "Summerhill." by Neill. Dane who was studying to be a teacher in the early 1970's wrote it. Though I personally did not read the Summerhill book, I concluded that the author was a liberal teacher who might smile, as he was being kicked in the shins by one of his students, only to say, "Johnnie, that is not acceptable behavior."

Dane wrote in part: "I must admit, while slowly reading Summerhill, my thinking underwent countless changes as I absorbed the material and experimented with it in both my personal life and in my classroom. I agree with Neil's goals, but at the same time often find myself objecting to his procedure. As I will illustrate throughout this paper – Neil's radical approach is not the only way, and perhaps not the best. I suppose that it is natural that I'll refer to myself much of the time, for of whom else am I more qualified to speak."

The author stated within the text, "Civilization is sick and unhappy, and I claim the root of it is the un-free family." Dane's written response was: "Well I object, as I am sure my parents would. Neil's deliberations seemingly compensate for all existing sickness and unhappiness, but what of those of us who <u>do</u> experience a feeling of adjustment and happiness and peace of mind? I am a product of the "un-free family." It is fact that my parents were quite strict with my two younger brothers and myself. For example, my father was quite rigid about the length of my hair. Another is the fact that I wasn't permitted to drive an automobile alone until I was seventeen. They felt it better that I obtain some experience after finishing driver's education. They were quite sincere and open in their beliefs, and entirely concerned that I understand the reasoning behind a particular way of thinking. Most of their reasoning made sense to me, thus I experienced no hate, no unhappiness, but rather a respect and forthright love. As for the reasoning I didn't understand – even parents are human, and I was capable of realizing this. My parents have not claimed to never had made mistakes, only to do the best they could. Neil says, "A loving environment, without parental discipline will take care of most of the problems of childhood." He goes on to say, "If children are given an environment of love and approval in the home, without parental discipline, nastiness, hate and destructiveness will never arise." My parents offered environs of love and approval as well as discipline, and I have yet to experience nastiness, hate, and destructiveness. I am curious as to how Neil would explain this. He has failed to compensate for my home and others like it. "The proper home" says Neil, "is the home in which children and adults have equal rights." My home fails to fit in any of these categories. Equal rights didn't exist. What existed was an understanding that perhaps my parents knew best. This understanding was backed by the feeling that whatever I might have to say on a particular matter would be carefully considered."

Other segments of the paper will be omitted in the interest of brevity, but I am certain we can get the picture formed in our young son's mind. Finally here is the final paragraph in the essay, and the words that tell it all about this particular son that we raised. Dane stated, "The normally constituted child just doesn't require the freedom Summerhill has to offer. As evidence, *I submit myself.*"

What more can a Dad ask for? Dane, married to Connie, also a teacher, is now 53 years old, and resides on Lookout Mountain near Chattanooga, Tennessee. Daughter Holly recently made them grandparents and simultaneously made us great-grandparents. He has had a stunning career in education and currently is the Curriculum Advisor for the Walker County school system in Georgia. How ironic!

MARK - Here's an Email received 03 November 2002 from Mark, our number 2 Son. Wow!

"Hi Dad,

I'm heading home from Bangkok Thailand tomorrow, hoping the plane isn't too overbooked. I was daydreaming a bit last night, which is one of my favorite things to do when I'm on vacation and have no phone and mental interruptions. Remember when you taught us how to climb small trees and ride them down to earth, while holding on for dear life? Mom never quite approved of that but it was exciting and fun! The smell of crisp bacon and smoky toast cooked over a fire in the woods on one of our many beloved breakfast hikes. I always loved to fly in the little Beechcraft Bonanza, but couldn't enjoy myself until I threw up because of "the smell." I think I decided to get "airsick" while on the runway and get it over with. What a strange circle.... Later an Air Force fighter pilot, now I get goose bumps and my heart smiles when I smell the sickly, sweet burning JP4 from a jet engine, or see the F-4 Phantom that I loved and miss so much. I remember going to classes at church to gear up to go before the elders and tell them why I wanted to be a member. At all of about 12 or 13, I told you I didn't want to be a church member and would feel like a hypocrite. Wisely, you said I might be a bit young to make such a decision, and "just do it" but speak my mind. I'll never forget the look on the elders when I told them I didn't want to join, but my parents felt I should and I had some burning doubts about all this religion business. Later, the elders told Mom that my talk was the best of the bunch - sincere and from the heart instead of canned pabulum. Nobody believes me when I tell him or her about our swimming kitty-cat, or coaxing a small rattlesnake into a catsup bottle - stories, nor that Bud Timm and I actually saw a not-of-this-earth UFO. So I quit telling those stories (except to you).

It's great to say that you're my Dad, and I love being your son. Love, Mark"

Now age 50, Mark resides in Victorville California and owns over 100 houses that he rents to people. An ex USAF F4 fighter jock and Instructor Pilot who graduated from the Air Force Academy has motivated him to continue traveling the world several times each year. He has yet to marry. As Mark puts it, "I'm still looking for someone like Mom!"

GREG – our 45-year-old number 3 Son as a youngster did not adapt as easily to the strict Ward family discipline, as his other two brothers. Keeping him walking a straight line became a parental challenge that we were able to meet, and it all worked out in the end and we are extremely proud of this young man. It is a distressing fact that Greg's real talents were not properly recognized while he attended school. Academic endeavors came in a far second to constructing airplane models, designing iceboats and other crafts that he could accomplish with his creative mind and coordinated hands. His obsession for precision, craftsmanship, perfectionism and thinking in the abstract were not truly appreciated nor developed by his teachers during the early school years, but immediately thereafter he enlisted into Naval Aviation for the next six years of his life. It was there that his talents and leadership capability blossomed. Having personally seen his military records, I can vouch for the fact that he made straight 4.0's during his complete tour of duty and received many awards. After his Navy tour he then attended the same school as myself, namely Pittsburgh Institute of Aeronautics then joined the staff of the Kalamazoo Aviation History Museum, (AirZoo) where he is currently their "Senior Curator of Aircraft Restoration." To describe the magical work that Greg and the large team of volunteer craftsmen perform in these restorations is impossible. Envision something that is perfect in your mind's eye then try to improve on that vision. Get the idea? There are few jobs that one can devote the necessary time to work in the realm of perfectionism, but Greg's got one of them. When he announced his marriage to Theresa around our dinner table in 1990, I queried her as to how she thinks she might put up with a perfectionist. Her comment – "Well, I'm going to give it my best shot." That she has, as has our nine-year-old Granddaughter Victoria, who by the way has her own handcrafted chest of tools, and already is expressing multifaceted talents shrouded in perfectionism. Is it any wonder?

I look at Greg and see a reflection of myself in my early years when I embraced my actions with non-academic skills and perfectionism. Along the way, we who follow that path have to learn to live with compromise, lest it drives us crazy. I made this transition, and I see Greg following a similar path and for that we are even more proud.

DONNA THE SINGER!

From time to time, things occur that fill my life with joy. They reinforce the fact that we were correct in the way we raised our kids and that God blessed our marriage, in spite of my own stumbling from time to time. There are so many things that can be said about Donna and the kids, that it would take volumes.

My bride is a well-known vocalist whose primary passion has been performing classical and religious music throughout her life. It took some doing to sidestep her into this category of music, but I had always wanted her to record an album of contemporary songs. The mechanics of going forward with the project, however, were a stumbling block. This changed rapidly when in early 2003 just by chance, I bumped into musical artist Rendal Wall, son of the famous Rem Wall, who played with the "Green Valley Boys." I was personally acquainted with Rem many years ago through our common interest in aviation. Rendal, called 'Ren' by his friends is also a pilot, so the common bond of flying seems to have been the thread that stitched the fabric of progress. Ren's involvement as a musical artist is a fascinating story, highlighted, by his background with the Gibson Guitar Company and more recently with the famous Heritage Guitar, Inc. Company, located in Kalamazoo, Michigan.

When Ren heard Donna's musical ability, he promptly said, "Do it!" followed by "I have a musician friend in Kalamazoo who has one of the 'best ears' in the industry, and he may take on the project. Would you like to meet him?" Meet him we did, and professional artist Neil Harding took on the project of arranging the music and recording, so my dream might be realized.

"Feelings," "Old Black Magic," "Girl From Ipanema", "Baubles Bangles & Beads," "Laura," and of course "Come Fly With Me" are but a few of the songs recorded on Donna's CD, labeled "Reflections – Songs for the young at heart". What started out to be a means of documenting Donna's beautiful voice has turned into a fun and profitable venture. She sure made me proud of her, by reaching out and spicing up our life with this project.

If you would like to hear a few free samples of "Reflections" on your computer, go on the web, click on the search button then type in Donna Ward. You can even order one for yourself with a couple of clicks and a credit card.

Donna Ward's commercial CD
R. Ward Collection

RIP TIDE, A LESSON LEARNED –

My mind continues to be drawn to the many events that involved the boys. One such event that involved two of them reminds me of the fragility of life to this very day.

In all of my flying years, I have never experienced a "brush with death" that even comes close to that which occurred on a sunny day many years ago along the sandy beaches of Georgia. Here was an experience I normally block from my mind, yet I bring it forth as a valuable lesson in how self-discipline can save ones life. The time frame involved was a period of very heavy business periods for me in the early years of my company. Frequent traveling and tight schedules created shortages in the quality time that I could devote to our boys. It was this fact that enticed me into taking our two older Sons - Dane, 13 and Mark, 9 years old, along with me on an impromptu trip to the southern states to call on one of our warehouse distributors. About 2:00 PM, the Boys were alerted and an hour or so later we were airborne in our company Beechcraft. The first stop would be near Sea Island, Georgia, where we checked into the King & Prince Hotel. Having lived on our Michigan inland lake for many years, and all of us being enthusiastic swimmers, we looked forward to the inviting surf.

After my business call was completed during the next afternoon, we donned our swimsuits and went out on the beach directly in front of the hotel. Mark, who was an avid sea shell collector pointed to a reach of land a few hundred feet off shore, connected by a ribbon of clear blue rather shallow water. At low tide, according to a couple of the locals, shells were abundant on that sandy strip. They were simply waiting for our discovery. With the tide on the way out, and becoming quite low, it seemed perfectly reasonable to wade to the reef, as it became more and more visible. The going was very easy. In fact, too easy. Side by side, we treaded in the water toward the reef. Only after noting that Mark, the youngest boy was bouncing off of the bottom with his toes, did I realize that the bottom was dropping off to a point that would be over his head. Swimming that distance was no problem for myself, but the boys were not that accomplished. In the span of a few seconds, both boys were swept outward and away from me. A lunge allowed me to grab Dane and in turn I demanded verbally that he grab Mark's hand, and hold on tight. Having dealt with the sea as an ex-Navy man and with considerable SCUBA diving experience through the years, I was acutely aware of the ocean's reaction to weakness. If alone, I would have used the time-honored technique of swimming parallel to the shoreline, until the rip tide current subsided but with the boys in hand my best judgment said to head back to shore.

The few persons on the beach were oblivious to our situation. Help was simply not available. To the boys way of thinking, this was fun, yet I knew enough about panic to treat this set of circumstances in a manner that would enable them to keep the right train of thought. An invisible and treacherous force that never presented its true colors had suddenly become our master. Every inch I made toward shore with the boys in trail was brutally resisted by the rip tides invisible force. We stayed as a group, with Mark the youngest now swimming about as much underwater as he was on top, but still in control. We made no headway, but with maximum exertion, we could stay in the same spot. The bottom now lost from sight, brushed by my feet once in a while. "Stay together boys, I'll work us back in." My muscles ached. The salt taste was getting to me. A plan – I needed a plan. We were starting to loose ground. If only I could touch bottom! Then it came to me in a flash. Why not touch bottom. Under I went, still tightly holding Dane's hand and he Mark's. My toes touched the bottom and I dug them into the sand. The rip tide resisted my stubbornness. An incredible feeling, it seemed that the pull pulsated. In a plan provided to my mind that could have possibly been the work of the Lord, in a series of movements conducted in sequence, I found the strength and ability to beat the deadly rip tide. One: Swim against the tide's outward pull. Two: Go underwater and grab the sand with my toes, holding on until the "pulse" subsides for a moment. Three: Lunge forward on the bottom toward the shore. It worked! Foot by foot over what seemed like an eternity, I gained solid footing, to a point where the boys could also touch bottom and play the same game with the vicious sea. Desperately fatigued, we dragged ourselves up on the beach. The few people around didn't even know that a life and death game had been in progress. A call for help would have probably done harm by adding to a panic possibility.

I've never spoken again to the boys about this experience. I wonder when they read this, if they will relate to it in any more detail than simple youthful fun? I think I'll ask them.

DON'T EVER LOSE YOUR SENSE OF HUMOR. IT'S AN ASSET GREATER THAN MONEY

As a young businessman in the early 1950's, I used to stop by the bank from time to time almost always in my tattered work clothes. As I passed his office, I would always utter a snide comment to Mr. Renshaw, the local First National Bank Vice President whom I really respected. Keep in mind that during that phase of my life, we were never hungry but we operated on an almost nonexistent budget. Nevertheless, Mr. Renshaw always spoke a friendly word and even though we did not have a pot to pee in would constantly remind me in jest that he would wait until I was wealthy and at that time would make some real big bucks off me. I would respond with a typical remark such as "I sure wish that you would come to work looking like the rest of us common folks, instead of playing the part of a banker." The messages changed from time to time but the exchanges always broke the monotony of our busy day. At the end of one of our verbal harpooning sessions, with my back already turned to him, Mr. Renshaw called out, "Dick, *don't you ever lose your sense of humor. It's an asset greater than money.*" Truer words were never spoken and to this day I have never lost my sometimes-warped sense of humor. It is in this spirit that I pass some happenings on to you. If you don't have a sense of humor of your own, loosen up and acquire one then never loose it. It will serve you well and get you through some rough times. By the way, Mr. Renshaw passed on before he was able to witness my accumulation of our modest personal financial wealth; therefore he was never able to make the big bucks from me. I do feel however that my occasional verbal game playing with him in some small way enhanced his life. It sure enhanced mine, and I continue to hone my own sense of humor. Here are a couple examples.

Relief Tube Improvement - You may recall what a "relief tube" is from an earlier chapter? If not, envision a plastic funnel, affixed to a hose normally stationed out of view under the lower front of a pilot's seat in the cockpit. It's a handy thing to have on a long flight. The opposite end of the hose is attached to a small venturi tube that is attached to the <u>bottom</u> of the fuselage. The venturi creates a suction that enables the fluid to disperse into the air-stream as the relieving experience takes place.

A number of months ago, our local Fixed Base Operator was requested to make a relief tube installation on a friend's Beechcraft Twin Bonanza. I supplied them with the materials and instructions to do so. When I stopped by their shop on the way to my own hangar, I stopped by to see what progress had been made, only to find that the venturi was mounted on the top of the fuselage directly in front of the windshield. I later discovered that the installation was dummied up with double-edged tape to make me think that it was real. That's a classic example of a mechanic with a sense of humor! Not to be outdone, I grabbed my digital camera and shot a photo of the installation, after which I made up an official letter of application for approval complete with photographs. Showing this wonderful advancement in the state of the art, as you will discover, now had a multiple purpose. I then mailed the "official" packet off to our local FAA Flight Service District Office (FSDO). I also sent a copy to a friend who is a senior engineer in the FAA engineering section of the FAA. He immediately came back with a suggestion indicating that he was concerned about the possibility of an opaque film being formed over the windshield. He stated that I should have included a "placard" to be place on the instrument panel that includes certain specific language. I immediately designed this addendum in compliance with his suggestion and forwarded it on to our FSDO office. It states;

THE PILOT IN COMMAND, PRIOR TO EACH FLIGHT WITH A PLANNED DURATION OF OVER ONE HOUR MUST DRINK AN ADEQUATE AMOUNT OF STRAIGHT GIN OR VODKA BEFORE EACH FLIGHT, SO THAT THE URINE COLOR WHEN EXPELLED IN THE RELEIF TUBE WILL

BE SUBSTANTIALLY CLEAR, THEREBY PREVENTING YELLOW ICE FROM FORMING ON THE WINDSCREEN AND OBSTRUCTING HIS VIEW.

I figured this would give the FAA guys some fun and break up the monotony of their otherwise regimented days. Of course, I did not expect to hear back from the FSDO office but a couple of months later I discovered that our local FBO owner, John Conrad, was expecting a visit from two FAA inspectors for the purpose of inspecting his repair station. I mentioned to John that I wanted him to have these guys stop by my hangar so that I could chastise them for not approving my relief tube application. I was prepared to lay into them pretty hard in jest and wallow further in my fun. Unfortunately I discovered that they cut and ran, even though John told them that I wanted to see them. When John noted to them that I was "unhappy" about not having heard back from them about my data package being approved, one of the inspectors - the older one, kind of smiled and said nothing. The younger guy muttered a few words and indicated that my application actually got into the FAA computer and the regional FAA office actually sent some one over to "counsel" the offending FAA inspector. *I love it!*

Radical new design of Relief Tube Venturi for windshield
ice prevention
R. Ward Collection

A sense of humor can literally work for you. Tilson (Til) Peabody was the head of the Detroit General Motors Flight Department in 1950's. I got to know Til on a personal level when I became president of the Michigan Aviation Trades Association (MATA). Those were the days when GM's fleet was larger than many airlines by operating something close to 20 aircraft including DC3s and Convairs to service their executives and customers. They were also the pre-computer days when flight plan trip strips were slid along from one controller to the other in the towers and air traffic control centers.

Having the responsibility of providing a speaker to our Rotary Club, I decided to see if Til would consider traveling to Three Rivers to present a program on executive flying. Without hesitation, he accepted my offer and ultimately flew into our small field in one of the GM DC3's. I was elated to be able to present this dynamic aviation legend to our local club members, especially when I was working so hard in the community to tout the advantages of our airport to the community.

Til explained how the scheduling system worked among other things but brought to our attention just how difficult it was for their pilots to schedule departure times with the executives. He noted that there were always the stragglers that made it difficult for the crews to file their flight plans for departure at some appointed time, then keep the flight plan alive to prevent re-filing. How well I understood this dilemma, having been a victim of this myself many times in my charter pilot days. Now we have a couple of hours before the Instrument flight plan drops out of the FAA computer. Back then, the time continually had to be updated by phone over and over again while waiting for the passengers.

Til stated that he had finally had about enough so he decided to issue an internal memo to all of the GM aircraft users. As he read it out loud from a note the he had in his hand, it went something like this:

From: Tilson Peabody/ Director, Flight Operations
To: GM Air Transport users
Cc: GM Flight crews
Subject: Flight departure times; New procedure

Our crews have brought forward an issue that I feel requires attention. It involves departure times.

Each flight requires that they file a flight plan with Air Traffic Control in which they provide a small window of time before and after the selected departure time. When this time arrives, the crew must continually update this time over and over via telephone. There is also the possibility that late departures could interrupt the balance of scheduling for the day.

By issuing this new procedure, I believe that it will greatly enhance the efficiency of our flight department:

1. The executive originating the trip will schedule the departure time with our scheduling department.
2. Upon arrival at the destination, the originator will communicate with the plane captain and establish an agreed-upon return departure time.
3. The originator will coordinate this time with his/her people.
4. The crew will file their departure flight plan based upon this time estimate.
5. When the appointed time arrives, the crew will prepare for departure.
6. In the event that the originator and/or those traveling with him/her do not show up at the appointed hour the crew will move the departure time later one-half hour.
7. In the event that the originator and/or those traveling with him/her still have not shown up at this extended time, *the crew will continue to wait until they get there.*

I queried Til after the meeting as to whether or not he actually dispersed this memo and he stated that he actually did so. He indicated that for the most part it did wonders to cure the problem. Now that is humor used in a sophisticated form!

A sense of humor – If you don't have one,
you are to be pitied
By: Author

SOMETIMES WE LEARN IN STRANGE WAYS

The year was 1965 when I had a call informing me a new FAA inspector had just taken over in the South Bend FAA FSDO office to monitor all FAA approved repair stations in their jurisdiction. To be candid, I generally looked upon these guys with suspicion when they called, as I had never seen what they could do to improve my company other than to come up with ridiculous governmental regulation interpretations that were often used to advance their own egos. My technique was to always give them the time of day but to never allow myself to become a victim of their time wasting idiosyncrasies. This episode falls within that category. To my way of thinking, not much has changed to this day. I hasten to point out however that there are certainly exceptions within the FAA organization that should not be painted broad brush. I know who the good guys are and so do they. 'Nuf said'!

I had no idea what he wanted to talk about in detail, beyond the fact that he mentioned something about the "Wind Driven Generator" that we had been producing since the 1950's. I decided to get him started on the right foot.

Judy Wallace, my great secretary, showed the inspector into my office and sat him directly in front of my large beautiful solid walnut "Dumore" desk that I had recently purchased. This desk is one of the assets that I did not sell along with the company. It represents the first thing I purchased in my life of an extravagant nature after I could afford to do so.

I had already cleared off my desk completely and in the middle of the bare desk placed my Dictaphone. When Blacker started to talk, I told him to hold it a minute, picked up the microphone, pressed the button and noted the details of the meeting including the date and our names. Set on conference position, I set the microphone in the middle of the table and promptly advised him to start speaking. "Why are you doing that?" he declared. When I pointed out that it is my personal procedure to do so, there was no small talk and he proceeded to present what he considered to be some sort of a problem.

The "problem" as he envisioned related to some Mickey Mouse idea that he dreamed up to create a lot of paperwork for us. To give you some understanding, one of my original products, a Wind Driven Generator kit, consisted of the generator, voltage regulator and universal mounting kit plus detailed installation instructions that included a blanket FAA approval letter. Each installation was unique to the specific aircraft and would be approved by the mechanic sending in a form 337 Repair & Alteration form. This system worked quite well for many years and was an easy process for our customers. The inspector got the bright idea that I should provide the FAA engineering drawings for each and every make and model on which the kit was installed. Just the thought of this prompted me to pick up my Dictaphone microphone and state that we would not even consider his proposal, and that the meeting was over. I asked Judy to show him the door.

Other FAA people would occasionally come around but that particular Inspector never came around. A couple of years later, I ultimately heard that he had been moved to the Central Regional FAA office in Chicago and was promoted as head honcho over all of the Approved Repair Station activity within the region.

Fast forward to the mid 1970's, when Judy rang me on my office phone and said that there was an FAA inspector in the lobby asking to see me on a personal matter and that it was a personal visit. Judy showed him in. He started the conversation with "You probably don't remember me but we previously met. I was passing through and wanted to mention something to you." Indeed I did remember him and I repeated his name. He reminded me of our meeting a number of years prior and followed with this statement: "Mr. Ward, you probably think that I hate your guts for the way you blew me off during our one and only meeting, but I want you to know that I was off base and you taught me a valuable lesson". He then handed me his business card and said that if there was anything that he could ever do for me, to just give him a call. He had also written down his home number on the card. A little discussion followed as he excused himself. We shook hands as he departed and I commented to him that it took a real man to go out of his way to understand how a small businessman thinks when it comes to dealing with a bureaucracy. I really appreciated the fact that he went out of his way to make this known.

I looked at his business card and noted that he was now based in the Washington DC FAA office and was the chief inspector overseeing all of the FAA Repair Stations in the nation.

I did impose on him a couple of times, when I felt that some new shooter came forth with a stupid interpretation of the regulations, and that would be the end of that. We stayed in touch until he retired and I have since heard that he has "gone west."

I'm from the Government and I'm here to help you.
By: Author unknown

EVER HAVE THE MOB ON YOUR HEELS?

The Pacific Club in Kalamazoo, Michigan was one of several places that served liquor by the glass in the 1950's. Those who did were all private clubs at that time. It was one of the hangouts for the "village idiots," as I termed them. I would occasionally receive a call to meet them and eat lunch prior to charter flying them up to Beaver Island, where their boozing would continue. The Pacific Club was unique, insofar as the majority of the clientele was very upscale, classy, and Black. However Whites were admitted and their patronage encouraged. I believed the Pacific Club to be way ahead of the time since when one joined the club, all members Black or White, were required to sign an affidavit as part of the application agreeing there would be no animosity between the black and white race and all would coexist in harmony. I saw no problem with this and from what I witnessed, this absolutely was the case; and mutual respect existed. The owner's name was Council Hall, a tall Black gentleman who really did a good job managing this elite club with its beautiful decor. Their food was outstanding and though I did not indulge, it was easy to see that the drinks were poured generously. It was always a pleasure for me to get the opportunity to get a free meal with the check being signed by one of my airplane charter clients during those days when we could hardly afford our humble living expenses.

Rumor had it that Chicago mob money was behind this organization, and there were other goings on. If there were those who actually knew, it was never shared with me. There was the mysterious upstairs of the two-story building adorned by the wide railed staircase on one side of the building interior. Though often spoken about, no one that I knew ever seemed to really know what was going on upstairs. Adding to this intrigue was an interesting focal point that was mounted above the highly visible main bar. A well engineered group of mirrors were slanted at a 45-degree angle so that virtually anyone one who sat at the bar or even the tables surrounding the bar had a clear view directly down the bosoms of some finely dressed ladies who sipped their martinis whilst sitting on the padded bar stools. Was it part of the architectural design or an interesting coincidence? Who cares? The effect was the same.

One evening, I received a call at home from Council Hall requesting that I fire up the airplane in the morning and take he and one of his friends to Saint Louis, Missouri. He stated that it was time to purchase all new furniture for the club and that one of his clients by the last name of Havey had a big-time connection with a restaurant furniture manufacturing company in East St. Louis and could get him new booths and other interior items at cost. He indicated that Havey had been very good to him and had even donated an expensive original painting that hung on the wall of his establishment. Early the next morning he and Havey showed up on time and we winged our way to St. Louis, landing at Lambert field. They rented a car and invited me to go along.

After being introduced to the owner and directed to the showroom, Council picked out some elegant and expensive booths and signed a deal. For those who are not aware of the fact, East St. Louis was a hotbed of crime and prostitution in those days and not a place that one would wish to bring up their kids. Since we had completed our business fairly early, Havey, who was from this neighborhood but had moved to Kalamazoo, said that he would "show us around" the neighborhood as well as a closed nightclub that he apparently used to either own or run. Off we went! When we arrived at the nightclub, he opened the door and showed us around, and then in a very short time we headed back to Lambert field, took off and put back down in Kalamazoo. With a single exception, that would be the end of the story.

A few weeks later, I picked up a Kalamazoo Gazette newspaper. Staring at me on the front page was a picture of Council's friend Havey, being led away in handcuffs by the police. He was just arrested a day before by the cops while stealing a wealthy persons jewelry and expensive paintings. He was caught in the act. I immediately called Council Hall to see what else he knew. He said – "Dick, you don't know the half of it. When we got back from St. Louis, I had a phone call from a friend in Chicago who asked me if I knew who the hell I was associating with when I drove around East St. Louis with a guy named Havey?" Council elaborated by saying that he probably should not mention this to me, but he thought that I should be aware of the fact that Havey had been run out of East St. Louis by the mob and that he had a contract out on him. Apparently the word had spread that he was in town and while we were there some hitmen were on our tail as we drove from place to place. The mob apparently did not know that Havey was in Kalamazoo but they undoubtedly would find out after someone sent them a newspaper clipping. Council also told me that he pulled the expensive painting off of the Pacific Club wall and mumbled about some other gifts that were provided. Where they went, I'll never know, nor did I ever feel as though I wanted to know.

A couple of years later, the Pacific Club burned to the ground and I have no idea where Council Hall might have gone. Hmmm!

WRITE-OFF DAYS

Do you experience certain days when the pressure seems to be more than you can endure? If you have not, you're a robot. I have no idea how I stumbled upon this solution but can tell you that it has served me well. Try it. If it works for you, immediately mail me an autographed dollar, so I can prove my point to my friends.

To put it in simple terms, each time you get the feeling that your lid will blow off because of all of the compounded problems that are occurring on a specific day, make an admission to yourself. Declare in your mind and verbally shout it out to yourself, "This is a Write-off Day," then forget about it. All of the ranting and raving in the world won't fix the problem. It is the specific day that is causing all of the grief and not the mess we think we're in. I don't know how they are scheduled, but I sure know that can sneak up on us.

I honestly believe that there are such days. I further believe that the next day provides us with a fresh outlook and it will not only be bearable, but actually better. We are all entitled to a certain number of write-off days. They exist, and all we have to do is recognize them and declare them as a way to make things better.

151

Richard I. Ward

WE INFLUENCE OTHER LIVES MORE THAN WE REALIZE. LET US CHERISH THIS HONOR.

This fact was driven home to me a number of years ago in a real way, through the following event.

I received a call from our U. S. Congressman's office in 1987 asking for a favor. (Now that's a switch.) They were requesting that I consider giving a ride in my 1942 Ryan ST open cockpit aircraft to a 92-year-old gentleman from Sturgis, Michigan. Clyde (Hoopy) Hoopingarner was a pilot in 1917 during World War I, and had never had his hands on the controls since that time. Of course, I told them, I would be honored to do so and to set up a time when we could meet at the Three Rivers Airport.

The day arrived and both the Sturgis and Three Rivers newspaper reporters were on hand to greet and interview him when he arrived. I had already briefed them on the fact that once in the air I would circle over his home in Sturgis and also pointed out that I would let him take the controls while doing so. We all wondered what the fellow would look like and assumed that he might arrive hobbling along with a cane or even worse, in a wheelchair. A car pulled up to the small terminal building and the single occupant promptly got out of the driver's seat and strolled into the lobby. It was my passenger.

During the interview with the media persons, he displayed a number of items that he had saved through the years; his silk scarf, flight jacket and leather helmet with goggles. Inside his helmet there were the signatures of his flight school classmates.

We walked out to the Ryan and I positioned him in the front cockpit. After strapping him into his parachute, shoulder harness and seat belt, off we went. My Ryan has a small intercom system whereby I can speak to the person in the front cockpit but he/she can't speak back. I like it that way. Heading southeast to Sturgis, I advised that I was turning the controls over to him and he should shake the stick when he took over. I made a few comments about keeping the wings level and the nose on the horizon and said little more. He handled the aircraft with a reasonable amount of control, so much so, that I allowed him to fly all the way to Sturgis. When he found his house, he circled it twice and I told him to head back to

152

Three Rivers, which he immediately did. Before the landing I did a snap roll then completed the landing while allowing him to keep his hands on the stick and his feet on the rudder pedals. After parking the airplane we shook hands and bid each other farewell. That could be the end of the story except for the following.

A number of years later, Donna and I were in Florida, on the way to Costa Rica in our Beechcraft Twin Bonanza. We first had stopped in Titusville, Florida to visit with my old flying buddy, Bob Biggs, when a phone call came in asking for me. It was the Congressman's assistant. She somehow tracked me down because of a special event that I should know about. She stated that our old WW I friend had just peacefully passed away. He was discovered in the morning, sitting in his favorite chair with a full-page newspaper article of his last flight with me in the Ryan clutched in his hands. There was a paragraph in the article that quoted him as saying " It was beautiful!" the Sturgis native said after his half-hour flight over St. Joseph County. "Dick took me clear up there and God, it was beautiful!" There was another quote in the same article. 'Hoopy' stated – "A guy tried to sell me life insurance. I told him I'm not going to die." I agree Hoopy. You never will.

World War I pilot Clyde (Hoopy) Hoopingarner
touches the sky again at age 92
Three Rivers Commercial News photo

CHAPTER XI
FINAL LANDING

My mind is far too congested with words.
Some process keeps moving some of them forward to verbalize
with other human creatures as the need arises.
There is one word however that becomes more and more
commonplace while my life moves toward the setting sun. This
word gives me hours and hours of pleasure as it is sometimes
embraced and expanded upon allowing me to relive a lifetime of
experiences.
That word is "Flight."

By: Author

When does it all end…this flight through life's experiences? A flight so short that it must be compared in scope to a single grain of sand on the beaches of the universe. When does it all end? I'm convinced that it doesn't. My flights through this life with Donna at my side have simply been too enjoyable to declare that it will ever end. The last landing that I make no doubt about it will be a touch and go! The final takeoff from earth will take me to areas of the universe I have never witnessed.

For now alas, thoughts and reminiscing will have to do. As the guys in the Air Traffic Control Center query from time to time "How's the ride?" At this stage of my life, it couldn't be better. Will

155

the final takeoff and the ensuing flight be my best? With the grace of God, there is no question about it. With each flight I now make in the Ford Tri-motor, our Beech Twin Bonanza, or the Ryan ST, I can see the Lord's face as I peer through the windscreen more clearly than ever. What a wonderful view!

- THE BEGINNING -

ABOUT THE AUTHOR

Richard (Dick) Ward resides in Three Rivers, Michigan with his cherished wife of fifty-five years. Smitten by the aviation bug at a very young age, he purchased and restored his first airplane at the age of fifteen and in 1943 learned to fly seaplanes on the Allegheny River in Pittsburgh, Pennsylvania. His multifaceted aviation and diverse business experiences are well documented within the pages of his numerous published writings of the past.

His many articles have been presented in such publications as – The Rotarian, Industry Week, Business Insight, Business and Commercial Aviation, Aviation Mechanics Journal, Martin Mariner, Airport Services Management, Parents, Solidarity, Battery Man, American Home, Model Airplane News, Flying Models, Private Pilot, Grounds Maintenance, AOPA Pilot, Aero, Grit, and Journal of Small Business. For over twenty years he has written and published a quarterly newsletter for the "Twin Bonanza Association" – a successful aircraft type club that he continues to operate (see www. twinbonanza.com).

His first book, "Beechcraft Twin Bonanza – Craft of The Masters," now in its second printing is a book that well documents the history of the historic Beechcraft Model 50 series and the Military L23/U8 aircraft used in Vietnam.

Aviation Ratings include: Commercial, Instrument, Multi Engine, Flight Instructor – single and multi engine, Ford Trimotor FO5 Type Rating, Aircraft & Powerplant Mechanic and Aircraft & Powerplant Mechanic Instructor.

Printed in the United States
32285LVS00014B/19-24